MW01675320

Writers Edge
2025 EDITION

AUTHORSHIP REIMAGINED: NFTS AND BLOCKCHAIN ESSENTIALS

Multi-Award-Winning-Author
B Alan Bourgeois

NFT and Blockchain Essentials

NFT and Blockchain Essentials for Authors' Success

ISBN: 979-8-3484-5527-9

Publisher: Bourgeois Media & Consulting (BourgeoisMedia.com)

BOURGEOIS
MEDIA & CONSULTING

B ALAN BOUERGEOIS

STORYTELLING LITERACY & HERITAGE

Thank you for purchasing this limited edition book, offered in celebration of the author's 50-year milestone. Proceeds from your purchase support the Texas Authors Institute of History, a museum founded by the author in 2015, dedicated to preserving the legacy of Texas authors.

https://TexasAuthors.Institute

Dear Fellow Authors,

I'm delighted to introduce this book—and every guide in this series—as a short, easy-to-read resource designed to help you succeed in your writing journey. As writers, our true passion lies in creating stories, and I understand that delving into the business side of publishing might not be where we wish to spend most of our time.

That's why I've made a conscious effort to keep things simple and straightforward, focusing on practical advice without unnecessary fluff. You'll find that some concepts overlap between books, and that's intentional—to reinforce key ideas and ensure that whichever guide you pick up, you're equipped with valuable tools to enhance your success.

I genuinely hope you find these guides enjoyable and helpful. Your feedback means the world to me, and I look forward to hearing about your experiences and triumphs.

Happy writing, and here's to your continued success!

Introduction

In the rapidly evolving landscape of digital publishing, authors are constantly seeking innovative ways to protect their work, engage with their audience, and maximize their revenue. Blockchain technology and Non-Fungible Tokens (NFTs) have emerged as transformative tools that offer a myriad of opportunities for authors. From ensuring the authenticity of digital assets to automating royalty payments and creating new revenue streams, NFTs and blockchain are revolutionizing the way authors publish and monetize their works.

This book, "NFT and Blockchain Essentials for Authors' Success," is designed to guide authors through the complex yet exciting world of NFTs and blockchain technology. It provides a comprehensive overview of the benefits, best practices, and technical considerations involved in leveraging these technologies for digital publishing. Whether you are an established author or an emerging writer, this book will equip you with the knowledge and tools needed to navigate the digital frontier confidently.

We begin by exploring the fundamental concepts of authenticity and proof of ownership, demonstrating how NFTs provide a unique digital signature that guarantees the originality of your work. We then delve into the immutable records offered by blockchain technology, highlighting the importance of transparent and tamper-proof transaction histories.

The book also addresses practical aspects such as royalty tracking, limited editions, and enhanced interactivity, showing how smart contracts can automate royalty payments and enable the creation of exclusive digital collectibles. We emphasize the importance of fan engagement and global accessibility, illustrating how NFTs can help you connect with readers worldwide and build a loyal community around your work.

In addition to the creative and financial benefits, we cover critical best practices for ensuring legal and regulatory compliance, protecting intellectual property rights, and managing privacy and confidentiality. By understanding these aspects, you can safeguard your work and navigate the digital landscape with confidence.

The final sections of the book focus on the technical and operational considerations of using blockchain and NFTs. We discuss the importance of choosing the right platforms, managing scalability and transaction costs, and implementing robust backup and recovery mechanisms. The book concludes with a look at future opportunities, encouraging you to embrace continuous learning and adapt to the ever-changing digital landscape.

"NFT and Blockchain Essentials for Authors' Success" is not just a guide but a roadmap to help you thrive in the digital age. By leveraging the power of blockchain and NFTs, you can protect your intellectual property, engage with your audience in innovative ways, and explore new revenue models that were previously unimaginable. Welcome to the future of digital publishing.

Section One
Benefits of NFTs and Blockchain for Authors

1. **Authenticity**: NFTs provide a unique digital signature, ensuring the originality and authenticity of each electronic book. This technology can effectively combat plagiarism and copyright infringement issues, giving authors confidence that their work remains genuine and protected in the digital realm.
2. **Proof of Ownership**: Tokenizing electronic books as NFTs allows authors to establish verifiable proof of ownership. This can be crucial for maintaining control over their work and protecting intellectual property rights, providing a secure and transparent record of ownership.
3. **Immutable Records**: Blockchain technology offers an immutable ledger that records the entire transaction history of an NFT. This permanent and tamper-proof record is valuable for maintaining a transparent history of ownership and transactions, enhancing trust and accountability.
4. **Royalty Tracking**: Smart contracts on the blockchain can automate royalty tracking and distribution. Authors can receive direct, transparent, and instant payments whenever their NFT books are sold or accessed, eliminating intermediaries and ensuring fair compensation.
5. **Limited Editions and Collectibles**: NFTs can represent limited edition or collector's items, allowing authors to create exclusive versions of their electronic books. This scarcity can increase their value and appeal to collectors, potentially generating additional revenue streams.

6. **Resale Value**: NFTs enable authors to earn royalties even when their electronic books are resold in the secondary market. Smart contracts can be designed to automatically distribute a percentage of the resale value back to the original author, providing ongoing revenue opportunities.
7. **Enhanced Interactivity**: Blockchain technology can enable the integration of interactive features within electronic books. For example, authors can create NFTs that grant access to additional content, multimedia elements, or exclusive events, enhancing the reader's experience.
8. **Fan Engagement**: NFTs can foster a direct connection between authors and their fans. By offering unique digital collectibles, authors can engage with their audience, reward loyalty, and create a sense of community around their work.
9. **Global Accessibility**: Blockchain technology allows for easy and secure distribution of electronic books worldwide. NFTs can be purchased and accessed by anyone with an internet connection, eliminating geographical barriers and expanding an author's reach.
10. **Future Opportunities**: Embracing NFTs and blockchain technology positions authors at the forefront of a rapidly evolving digital landscape. By exploring these emerging technologies, authors can gain valuable insights, experiment with new revenue models, and potentially open up doors to novel opportunities.

Section Two: Best Practices for Authors Using NFTs and Blockchain

1. **Ownership and Intellectual Property Rights**: Authors should ensure they have the legal rights to tokenize and sell their works as NFTs. Verifying ownership and clearing any copyright or licensing issues is crucial to protect their intellectual property.
2. **Authenticity and Verification**: Authors should prioritize establishing the authenticity of their NFTs. This includes providing unique and verifiable metadata, such as details about the work, its creation process, and any associated rights. Authenticity ensures credibility and guards against plagiarism or counterfeiting.
3. **Platform Selection**: Authors should carefully choose the NFT marketplace or platform to mint and sell their NFTs. Factors to consider include reputation, user base, transaction fees, ease of use, and community engagement. Thorough research helps select a platform that aligns with the author's goals and target audience.
4. **Metadata and Additional Content**: Authors should enrich their NFTs with meaningful metadata. This can include descriptions, background information, artist statements, or supplementary content that adds value to the NFT and enhances the collector's experience. Well-curated metadata can contribute to the overall appeal and desirability of the NFT.
5. **Licensing and Usage Rights**: Authors should consider the licensing terms and usage rights associated with their NFTs. They can specify whether the NFT grants the purchaser the right to display, resell, or access additional content related to the work. Clear communication of these terms helps manage expectations and avoid potential conflicts.

6. **Pricing and Revenue Models**: Authors should determine the pricing strategy and revenue model for their NFTs. Factors to consider include the uniqueness of the work, its perceived value, market demand, and the author's objectives. Authors can experiment with fixed pricing, auctions, tiered offerings, or even ongoing royalties from secondary sales.
7. **Promotion and Marketing**: Creating NFTs is not just about minting; authors should actively promote their NFTs and engage with the community. Utilize social media, online forums, and newsletters to build awareness, communicate with collectors, and foster a supportive community around the NFTs.
8. **Community Engagement**: Authors should actively engage with collectors and the NFT community. Building relationships, responding to inquiries, and participating in discussions can generate interest, loyalty, and support. Nurturing a strong community around the NFTs can lead to increased exposure and long-term success.
9. **Legal and Tax Implications**: Authors should be aware of the legal and tax implications of creating and selling NFTs. Consult with legal and tax professionals to ensure compliance with relevant regulations and understand any obligations related to income, royalties, or ownership rights.
10. **Continuous Learning and Adaptation**: The NFT space is constantly evolving. Authors should stay informed about new trends, technologies, and market developments. Embrace a mindset of continuous learning, experimentation, and adaptation to seize new opportunities and stay ahead in the rapidly changing landscape.

11.

Section Three: Technical and Legal Considerations

1. **Understanding Blockchain Technology**: Authors should have a solid understanding of blockchain technology, including its decentralized nature, immutability, and transparency. Familiarizing themselves with the basics of blockchain will help authors make informed decisions and leverage the technology effectively.
2. **Authenticity and Copyright**: Blockchain can provide a unique digital signature that ensures the originality and authenticity of electronic books. Authors should be diligent in verifying ownership and ensuring they have the necessary rights to publish their works on the blockchain. Clearing any copyright or licensing issues is crucial to protect their intellectual property.
3. **Tokenization**: Authors can consider tokenizing their electronic books as Non-Fungible Tokens (NFTs) on the blockchain. Tokenization enables the creation of unique digital assets that can represent ownership or access to specific electronic books. Authors should understand the tokenization process and the benefits it offers in terms of proof of ownership and verifiability.
4. **Privacy and Confidentiality**: Authors should be mindful of the privacy and confidentiality implications when using blockchain. Depending on the blockchain network chosen, some information may be visible to the public. Authors should assess the sensitivity of their content and evaluate whether private or permissioned blockchains are more suitable for their needs.
5. **Distribution and Access**: Blockchain technology enables easy and secure distribution of electronic books. Authors should explore blockchain-based platforms or marketplaces that provide a user-friendly interface for readers to access their works. It's essential to consider

factors such as user base, ease of use, and discoverability when selecting a platform.

6. **Royalty Tracking and Payments**: Smart contracts on the blockchain can automate royalty tracking and distribution. Authors should leverage this feature to ensure transparent and instant payments whenever their electronic books are sold or accessed. Understanding how smart contracts work and customizing them to suit their specific royalty requirements is crucial.
7. **Scalability and Transaction Costs**: Authors should consider the scalability and transaction costs associated with blockchain networks. Depending on the chosen blockchain, there may be limitations on the number of transactions that can be processed efficiently. Authors should assess the scalability of the blockchain network to ensure it can handle the potential demand for their electronic books.
8. **Backup and Recovery**: While blockchain technology provides resilience against data loss or tampering, authors should still have backup and recovery mechanisms in place. It's important to have redundant copies of their electronic books stored securely to mitigate the risk of losing access to their works due to unforeseen circumstances.
9. **User Experience**: Authors should prioritize the user experience when utilizing blockchain for their electronic books. It's essential to ensure that readers have a seamless and intuitive experience when accessing and reading the books on blockchain platforms. User feedback and continuous improvement efforts can help enhance the overall user experience.
10. **Legal and Regulatory Considerations**: Authors should be aware of any legal and regulatory implications when using blockchain for their electronic books. Intellectual property rights, copyright laws, and data protection regulations may vary across jurisdictions. Seeking legal

advice to ensure compliance with relevant laws and regulations is crucial.

Contents

Section One
Benefits of NFTs and Blockchain for Authors

1. Authenticity 16
2. Proof of Ownership 19
3. Immutable Records 22
4. Royalty Tracking 25
5. Limited Editions and Collectibles 28
6. Resale Value 30
7. Enhanced Interactivity 32
8. Fan Engagement 34
9. Global Accessibility. 36
10. Future Opportunities 39

Section Two:
Best Practices for Authors Using NFTs and Blockchain

1. Ownership and Intellectual Property Rights 43
2. Authenticity and Verification 46
3. Platform Selection 48
4. Metadata and Additional Content 50

5. Licensing and Usage Rights 53
6. Pricing and Revenue Models 56
7. Promotion and Marketing 59
8. Community Engagement 62
9. Legal and Tax Implications 64
10. Continuous Learning and Adaptation 67

Section Three: Technical and Legal Considerations

21. Understanding Blockchain Technology 71
22. Authenticity and Copyright 74
23. Tokenization 77
24. Privacy and Confidentiality 80
25. Distribution and Access 83
26. Royalty Tracking and Payments 86
27. Scalability and Transaction Costs 89
28. Backup and Recovery 92
29. User Experience 95
30. Legal and Regulatory Considerations 98
31. Continuous Learning and Adaptation 101
32. Future Opportunities 104

About the Author 107
Other Books by the Author in this Series 108

1
Authenticity

In the rapidly evolving landscape of electronic books, authors face various challenges, such as maintaining the originality of their works and protecting their intellectual property rights. Non-Fungible Tokens (NFTs) have emerged as a powerful solution, offering a unique digital signature that guarantees the authenticity and originality of each electronic book. In this chapter, we will delve into the significance of authenticity in the context of NFTs, exploring how they can combat plagiarism and copyright infringement issues.

The Power of NFTs in Ensuring Authenticity

NFTs, built on blockchain technology, provide an innovative mechanism to establish and verify the authenticity of digital assets, including electronic books. Each NFT represents a distinct, indivisible token that carries a unique digital signature. This digital signature serves as proof of ownership and authenticity, making it extremely difficult to replicate or tamper with.

By tokenizing electronic books as NFTs, authors can create an immutable record of their work. The blockchain ledger records the entire transaction history, from creation to ownership transfers, ensuring transparency and establishing a trustworthy chain of custody. This tamper-proof record serves as a powerful tool for authors to prove the originality and authenticity of their electronic books.

Combating Plagiarism and Copyright Infringement

Plagiarism and copyright infringement are pervasive issues in the digital content landscape. With the rise of easily accessible digital publications, authors often find their works copied, reproduced, and distributed without proper authorization. NFTs offer an effective solution to combat these issues:

1. **Unique Digital Signatures**: Each NFT associated with an electronic book carries a unique digital signature. This signature serves as a digital watermark, allowing authors and readers to verify the authenticity of the work. Any attempt to replicate or distribute the electronic book without the corresponding NFT would be immediately apparent, discouraging plagiarism and unauthorized copying.
2. **Traceability and Ownership Proof**: The blockchain ledger provides a transparent record of ownership transfers and transactions related to the NFT. This traceability enables authors to establish their ownership and rights over the electronic book. In case of copyright disputes, the blockchain record can serve as undeniable evidence of the original author's claim, making it easier to protect their intellectual property.
3. **Digital Rights Management**: NFTs can be accompanied by smart contracts that define and enforce specific usage rights. Authors can specify the terms of use, such as limitations on reproduction, distribution, and modification of the electronic book. Smart contracts enable automated enforcement of these rights, ensuring that the content remains protected and used in accordance with the author's intentions.
4. **Copyright Monetization**: NFTs can also facilitate new revenue streams for authors by enabling direct sales and royalties. When an NFT-protected electronic book is sold or accessed, the author can receive direct, transparent, and instant payments. This direct monetization model

bypasses intermediaries and ensures that authors are fairly compensated for their work, discouraging unauthorized copying that may harm their revenue potential.

The advent of NFTs and blockchain technology has brought about a paradigm shift in the way we establish and protect the authenticity of digital assets, including electronic books. By leveraging NFTs, authors can establish a unique digital signature for each electronic book, providing an indisputable proof of ownership and authenticity. This not only combats plagiarism and copyright infringement but also empowers authors to assert their rights and monetize their creations more effectively. As the digital landscape continues to evolve, embracing NFTs can be a pivotal step for authors to safeguard their work and thrive in an increasingly digital world.

2
Proof of Ownership

Ownership and control over one's work are fundamental rights that every author must safeguard. With the rise of digital publishing, the need for a secure and verifiable proof of ownership has become increasingly important. Tokenizing electronic books as NFTs provides authors with a robust mechanism to establish and maintain ownership of their intellectual property. This chapter explores how NFTs can serve as verifiable proof of ownership, ensuring that authors can protect their work and control its distribution.

The Role of NFTs in Establishing Ownership

NFTs, or Non-Fungible Tokens, are unique digital assets that represent ownership of a specific item or piece of content on the blockchain. When an author tokenizes their electronic book as an NFT, they create a digital certificate of ownership that is recorded on the blockchain. This certificate is immutable and publicly accessible, providing an undeniable proof of ownership that cannot be altered or disputed.

Benefits of Tokenizing Electronic Books as NFTs

1. **Verifiable Proof of Ownership**: The blockchain ledger records every transaction involving the NFT, creating a transparent and tamper-proof history of ownership. This record can be used to verify the author's ownership of the electronic book, providing a clear chain of custody from creation to current ownership.

2. **Protection of Intellectual Property**: By establishing a verifiable proof of ownership, authors can protect their intellectual property from unauthorized use or misappropriation. In case of a copyright dispute, the blockchain record serves as incontrovertible evidence of the author's rights.
3. **Enhanced Control Over Distribution**: NFTs enable authors to retain control over the distribution and use of their work. Authors can specify the terms of use in the smart contract associated with the NFT, ensuring that their work is used in accordance with their intentions.
4. **Revenue Opportunities from Secondary Sales**: NFTs can be programmed with smart contracts that automatically distribute royalties to the original author whenever the NFT is resold. This feature provides authors with ongoing revenue opportunities, allowing them to benefit from the increasing value of their work in the secondary market.

Case Study: Protecting Intellectual Property with NFTs

Consider an author who has written a popular science fiction novel. By tokenizing the novel as an NFT, the author creates a digital certificate of ownership that is recorded on the blockchain. This certificate includes metadata such as the book's title, publication date, and the author's information, providing a comprehensive record of ownership.

When the novel is sold as an NFT, the blockchain ledger records the transaction, creating a transparent history of ownership. If someone attempts to copy and distribute the novel without authorization, the author can point to the blockchain record as proof of their ownership and take appropriate legal action to protect their rights.

Additionally, if the NFT representing the novel is resold in the secondary market, the smart contract can ensure that a percentage of the resale value is automatically transferred to the original author, providing them with ongoing revenue from their work.

Tokenizing electronic books as NFTs provides authors with a powerful tool to establish and maintain ownership of their intellectual property. By creating a verifiable proof of ownership on the blockchain, authors can protect their work, control its distribution, and benefit from ongoing revenue opportunities. As the digital landscape continues to evolve, embracing NFTs can help authors safeguard their rights and thrive in an increasingly interconnected world.

3
Immutable Records

The integrity and security of records are paramount in the digital age, especially for authors who want to protect their intellectual property and maintain a transparent history of their work. Blockchain technology, with its immutable ledger, offers a revolutionary solution for recording and preserving the transaction history of NFTs. This chapter explores the concept of immutable records and how blockchain technology ensures a transparent and tamper-proof history for electronic books.

Understanding Immutable Records on the Blockchain

Blockchain technology is built on a decentralized and distributed ledger system, where each block contains a list of transactions. Once a block is added to the blockchain, it cannot be altered or deleted, making the record immutable. This immutability is achieved through cryptographic hashing, consensus mechanisms, and the decentralized nature of the blockchain network.

Benefits of Immutable Records for Authors

1. **Permanent and Tamper-Proof History**: The blockchain ledger records every transaction involving an NFT, creating a permanent and tamper-proof history. This ensures that the entire transaction history of an electronic book is transparent and cannot be altered or deleted, providing a reliable and trustworthy record.
2. **Enhanced Transparency**: The transparency of the blockchain ledger allows authors and readers to verify

the transaction history of an NFT. This transparency enhances trust and accountability, ensuring that the ownership and transfer history of an electronic book is clear and indisputable.

3. **Protection Against Fraud and Counterfeiting**: The immutability of the blockchain ledger protects against fraud and counterfeiting. Any attempt to alter the transaction history or create a counterfeit NFT would be immediately apparent, ensuring the integrity and authenticity of the electronic book.
4. **Simplified Dispute Resolution**: In case of a dispute over the ownership or transfer of an NFT, the immutable blockchain record serves as undeniable evidence. This simplifies dispute resolution and provides a clear and transparent record that can be used to assert ownership and protect intellectual property rights.

Case Study: Preserving the Transaction History of an Electronic Book

Consider an author who has tokenized their electronic book as an NFT and sold it to a collector. The blockchain ledger records the initial creation of the NFT, the sale transaction, and the transfer of ownership to the collector. Over time, the NFT may be resold to other collectors, with each transaction recorded on the blockchain.

Years later, if a dispute arises over the ownership of the electronic book, the author can refer to the blockchain record to verify the transaction history. The immutable record provides a transparent and tamper-proof history of ownership, making it easy to resolve the dispute and assert the author's rights.

Immutable records on the blockchain provide authors with a powerful tool to preserve the integrity and security of their work. By leveraging the transparency and immutability of the blockchain ledger, authors can maintain a permanent and tamper-proof history of their electronic books, protect against fraud and counterfeiting, and simplify dispute resolution. Embracing blockchain technology can help authors safeguard their intellectual property and build trust with their readers in the digital age.

4
Royalty Tracking

One of the most significant challenges authors face in the digital publishing world is ensuring they receive fair compensation for their work. Traditional royalty tracking and distribution systems often involve intermediaries, delays, and lack of transparency. Blockchain technology, with its smart contract capabilities, offers a solution to these issues by automating royalty tracking and distribution. This chapter explores how smart contracts can ensure transparent and instant royalty payments for authors.

The Role of Smart Contracts in Royalty Tracking

Smart contracts are self-executing contracts with the terms of the agreement directly written into code. They automatically execute and enforce the terms of a contract when predefined conditions are met. In the context of NFTs and electronic books, smart contracts can be used to automate royalty payments to authors whenever their books are sold or accessed.

Benefits of Using Smart Contracts for Royalty Tracking

1. **Transparency**: Smart contracts operate on the blockchain, providing a transparent and immutable record of all transactions. Authors can verify the sales and usage of their electronic books, ensuring they receive the correct royalties.
2. **Instant Payments**: Smart contracts can instantly execute royalty payments as soon as a sale or access transaction occurs. This eliminates delays associated with traditional

royalty distribution systems, ensuring authors are promptly compensated.

3. **Elimination of Intermediaries**: Smart contracts automate the royalty distribution process, removing the need for intermediaries such as publishers and collection agencies. This reduces costs and ensures that a larger share of the revenue goes directly to the author.
4. **Customizable Royalty Structures**: Authors can customize the terms of the smart contract to suit their specific needs. For example, they can set different royalty rates for primary sales and secondary market resales, ensuring they benefit from ongoing revenue opportunities.

Case Study: Automating Royalty Payments with Smart Contracts

Consider an author who has tokenized their electronic book as an NFT and sold it on a blockchain-based marketplace. The smart contract associated with the NFT specifies that the author will receive a 10% royalty on all primary sales and a 5% royalty on all secondary market resales.

When a buyer purchases the electronic book, the smart contract automatically transfers the royalty payment to the author's wallet. If the buyer later resells the NFT, the smart contract ensures that the author receives a 5% royalty from the resale transaction. This automated process ensures transparency, accuracy, and instant compensation for the author.

Smart contracts offer a revolutionary solution for royalty tracking and distribution in the digital publishing world. By leveraging the transparency and automation capabilities of blockchain technology, authors can ensure they receive fair and instant compensation for their work. Embracing smart contracts can help authors streamline their royalty management processes and maximize their revenue potential in an increasingly digital landscape.

5
Limited Editions and Collectibles

In the world of digital publishing, creating scarcity and exclusivity can significantly enhance the value of electronic books. NFTs provide authors with the ability to create limited edition or collectible versions of their works, attracting collectors and generating additional revenue streams. This chapter explores how authors can leverage NFTs to create and market limited edition and collectible electronic books.

Creating Limited Editions with NFTs

NFTs enable authors to create a finite number of digital copies of their electronic books, each represented by a unique token. This limited supply creates scarcity, increasing the perceived value of the work. Authors can choose to create a single edition or multiple editions with varying levels of exclusivity.

Benefits of Limited Editions and Collectibles

1. **Increased Value**: Limited edition NFTs can command higher prices due to their scarcity. Collectors are often willing to pay a premium for exclusive and rare digital assets.
2. **Enhanced Fan Engagement**: Offering limited editions allows authors to engage with their most dedicated fans, providing them with unique and valuable items that enhance their connection to the author's work.
3. **New Revenue Streams**: By creating and selling limited edition NFTs, authors can generate additional revenue beyond traditional sales. Collectible NFTs can appreciate

in value over time, providing ongoing revenue opportunities through secondary market sales.

4. **Creative Freedom**: Authors can experiment with different types of limited editions, such as illustrated versions, annotated editions, or multimedia-enhanced books. This creative freedom allows authors to offer unique and differentiated products to their audience.

Case Study: Launching a Limited Edition NFT Book

An author decides to launch a limited edition NFT version of their popular fantasy novel. They create 100 unique NFTs, each representing a digital copy of the book with exclusive illustrations and bonus content not available in the standard edition. The author prices each NFT at a premium, reflecting the scarcity and added value of the limited edition.

To promote the launch, the author leverages social media and engages with their fan community, highlighting the unique features and limited availability of the NFTs. The limited edition sells out quickly, generating significant revenue for the author and creating a buzz among collectors.

As the NFTs are resold in the secondary market, the author continues to earn royalties from each transaction, benefiting from the ongoing value of the limited edition.

Creating limited editions and collectibles with NFTs offers authors a powerful way to enhance the value of their electronic books and engage with their fans. By leveraging the scarcity and exclusivity of NFTs, authors can generate new revenue streams and offer unique and valuable products to their audience. Embracing this innovative approach can help authors stand out in the digital publishing landscape and maximize the potential of their creative works.

6
Resale Value

One of the unique advantages of NFTs is the ability to earn royalties from secondary market sales. Unlike traditional publishing, where authors typically receive royalties only from the initial sale, NFTs allow authors to benefit from the resale of their electronic books. This chapter explores how authors can leverage smart contracts to earn ongoing revenue from the resale value of their NFTs.

Understanding Resale Value with NFTs

NFTs are designed to be resold and traded in the secondary market. Each time an NFT changes hands, the transaction is recorded on the blockchain. Smart contracts can be programmed to automatically distribute a percentage of the resale value to the original author, ensuring they benefit from the continued demand for their work.

Benefits of Earning Royalties from Resales

1. **Ongoing Revenue**: Authors can earn royalties every time their NFTs are resold, providing a continuous stream of income. This ongoing revenue can significantly enhance the author's earnings over time.
2. **Increased Value**: As the resale value of an NFT increases, so does the royalty earned by the author. Authors benefit from the appreciation of their work in the secondary market.
3. **Incentive for Quality**: Knowing that they will earn royalties from resales, authors are incentivized to create

high-quality and desirable content that appeals to collectors and maintains its value over time.

4. **Enhanced Author-Reader Relationship**: Authors can maintain a connection with their readers and collectors through the resale process. This ongoing relationship can lead to increased loyalty and support for the author's future works.

Case Study: Earning Royalties from Secondary Market Sales

An author publishes an electronic book as an NFT and sells it to an initial buyer. The smart contract associated with the NFT specifies that the author will receive a 10% royalty on all secondary market resales.

Over the next few years, the NFT gains popularity and is resold multiple times. Each time the NFT is resold, the smart contract automatically transfers 10% of the resale value to the author's wallet. As the resale value increases, the author benefits from higher royalty payments, generating significant ongoing revenue.

The ability to earn royalties from secondary market sales is a game-changer for authors in the digital publishing world. By leveraging smart contracts and NFTs, authors can ensure they benefit from the continued demand for their work, providing a continuous stream of income and enhancing the value of their creative efforts. Embracing this innovative approach can help authors maximize their earnings and maintain a strong connection with their audience in the ever-evolving digital landscape.

7
Enhanced Interactivity

In the digital age, readers increasingly seek immersive and interactive experiences that go beyond traditional text. Blockchain technology and NFTs offer authors the opportunity to enhance the interactivity of their electronic books, creating engaging and dynamic content that captivates readers. This chapter explores how authors can leverage NFTs to integrate interactive features and provide a richer reading experience.

Integrating Interactivity with NFTs

NFTs can be used to unlock access to additional content and interactive features within electronic books. Authors can create NFTs that grant readers access to multimedia elements, exclusive events, and other engaging content that enhances the overall reading experience.

Benefits of Enhanced Interactivity

1. **Engaging Content**: Interactive features such as videos, audio clips, animations, and interactive maps can make the reading experience more engaging and enjoyable for readers.
2. **Added Value**: By offering additional content and interactive features, authors can increase the perceived value of their electronic books, making them more appealing to readers and collectors.
3. **Deeper Connection**: Interactive elements can create a deeper connection between the author and the reader, fostering a sense of immersion and involvement in the story.

4. **Monetization Opportunities**: Authors can monetize interactive features by offering them as exclusive content unlocked through NFTs, providing additional revenue streams.

Case Study: Creating an Interactive NFT Book

An author publishes an electronic book as an NFT, incorporating various interactive features. The NFT unlocks access to exclusive video interviews with the author, interactive maps of the book's setting, and bonus chapters with additional storyline content.

Readers who purchase the NFT can access these interactive features through a dedicated app or platform, enhancing their reading experience. The author promotes the interactive elements on social media and through their fan community, generating excitement and driving sales.

The interactive NFT book becomes a hit, attracting readers who are eager to explore the additional content and engage with the story in new and exciting ways. The author benefits from increased sales and revenue from the exclusive content.

Enhancing interactivity with NFTs offers authors a powerful way to engage readers and provide a richer, more immersive reading experience. By leveraging the capabilities of blockchain technology and NFTs, authors can create dynamic and interactive content that captivates their audience and increases the value of their electronic books. Embracing this innovative approach can help authors stand out in the digital publishing world and build a loyal and engaged readership.

8
Fan Engagement

Building a loyal and engaged fan base is crucial for the success of any author. NFTs provide a unique opportunity for authors to connect with their fans in meaningful ways, offering exclusive digital collectibles and fostering a sense of community. This chapter explores how authors can use NFTs to engage with their audience and create a supportive and enthusiastic fan base.

Fostering Fan Engagement with NFTs

NFTs can be used to create unique digital collectibles that appeal to fans and enhance their connection to the author's work. By offering exclusive items and experiences, authors can reward loyalty and build a strong sense of community around their books.

Benefits of Using NFTs for Fan Engagement

1. **Exclusive Collectibles**: Authors can create limited edition NFTs that represent unique digital collectibles, such as signed digital copies, special editions, and artwork. These exclusive items can attract collectors and dedicated fans.
2. **Direct Interaction**: NFTs can facilitate direct interaction between authors and their fans. Authors can offer NFTs that grant access to private events, Q&A sessions, and virtual meet-and-greets, providing fans with unique opportunities to connect with the author.
3. **Rewarding Loyalty**: By offering exclusive NFTs as rewards, authors can recognize and reward their most

loyal fans. This can include early access to new releases, exclusive content, and special merchandise.

4. **Community Building**: NFTs can help authors build a strong and supportive community around their work. Fans who own NFTs can participate in exclusive online forums, discussions, and events, fostering a sense of belonging and engagement.

Case Study: Engaging Fans with Exclusive NFTs

An author decides to create a series of exclusive NFTs to engage with their fan base. They offer limited edition digital copies of their latest book, each signed and numbered. Additionally, they create NFTs that grant access to a private online book club where the author participates in discussions and answers questions from fans.

To promote the NFTs, the author leverages social media and their email newsletter, highlighting the exclusivity and benefits of the digital collectibles. Fans eagerly purchase the NFTs, excited about the opportunity to own a unique piece of the author's work and participate in the private book club.

The author builds a strong and engaged community around their books, with fans actively participating in discussions and events. The NFTs become highly sought after, with resale value increasing in the secondary market, benefiting both the author and the fans who own them.

Using NFTs for fan engagement offers authors a powerful way to connect with their audience and build a loyal and enthusiastic fan base. By offering exclusive digital collectibles and unique experiences, authors can reward loyalty, foster community, and enhance their relationship with their readers. Embracing NFTs as a tool for fan engagement can help authors create a supportive and dedicated audience, driving long-term success in the digital publishing world.

9
Global Accessibility

The digital age has made it easier for authors to reach a global audience, but geographical barriers and distribution challenges still exist. Blockchain technology and NFTs provide a solution by enabling easy and secure distribution of electronic books worldwide. This chapter explores how authors can leverage NFTs to expand their reach and make their work accessible to readers around the globe.

Expanding Reach with Blockchain Technology

Blockchain technology allows authors to distribute their electronic books securely and efficiently to a global audience. NFTs can be purchased and accessed by anyone with an internet connection, eliminating geographical barriers and ensuring that readers from all over the world can enjoy the author's work.

Benefits of Global Accessibility

1. **Wider Audience**: By leveraging blockchain technology, authors can reach readers in different countries and regions, expanding their audience and increasing their potential readership.
2. **Secure Distribution**: Blockchain technology ensures secure and tamper-proof distribution of electronic books. Authors can protect their work from unauthorized copying and distribution, ensuring that readers receive genuine and authentic content.

3. **Cross-Border Payments**: NFTs facilitate cross-border payments, allowing authors to receive royalties and payments from readers worldwide. Smart contracts automate the payment process, ensuring transparency and instant compensation.
4. **Increased Discoverability**: Blockchain-based platforms and marketplaces provide a global stage for authors to showcase their work. Authors can increase their discoverability and attract readers from diverse backgrounds and locations.

Case Study: Reaching a Global Audience with NFTs

An author publishes their electronic book as an NFT on a blockchain-based marketplace. The NFT can be purchased and accessed by readers worldwide, with the blockchain ledger ensuring secure and transparent transactions.

To promote the book, the author engages with readers on social media, highlighting the global accessibility and benefits of the NFT. Readers from different countries purchase the NFT, excited about the opportunity to own a unique and authentic digital copy of the book.

The author receives payments directly through the smart contract, with royalties automatically distributed for each sale. The global reach of the NFT increases the author's readership and generates significant revenue from a diverse and international audience.

Leveraging blockchain technology and NFTs for global accessibility offers authors a powerful way to reach a wider audience and make their work accessible to readers around the world. By eliminating geographical barriers and ensuring secure distribution, authors can expand their reach, increase their discoverability, and benefit from cross-border payments. Embracing NFTs as a tool for global accessibility can help authors thrive in the digital age and connect with readers from diverse backgrounds and locations.

10
Future Opportunities

The digital landscape is rapidly evolving, and emerging technologies like blockchain and NFTs are opening up new possibilities for authors. Embracing these technologies positions authors at the forefront of innovation, allowing them to explore novel revenue models and creative opportunities. This chapter explores the potential future opportunities for authors in the NFT and blockchain space.

Exploring Future Opportunities with NFTs and Blockchain

As blockchain technology and NFTs continue to develop, authors can experiment with new ways to monetize their work, engage with their audience, and enhance their creative output. Staying informed about emerging trends and technologies can help authors seize new opportunities and remain competitive in the digital publishing world.

Potential Future Opportunities for Authors

1. **Innovative Revenue Models**: Authors can explore new revenue models such as subscription-based access to exclusive content, tiered pricing for different levels of engagement, and dynamic pricing based on demand and scarcity.
2. **Collaborative Projects**: Blockchain technology enables collaborative projects where multiple authors, artists, and creators can work together to produce unique and innovative content. NFTs can represent shared ownership and revenue distribution among collaborators.

3. **Interactive Storytelling**: The integration of interactive and multimedia elements within electronic books can create immersive storytelling experiences. Authors can experiment with augmented reality (AR), virtual reality (VR), and gamification to engage readers in new and exciting ways.
4. **Tokenized Communities**: Authors can create tokenized communities where fans and readers can participate in the creation and promotion of new works. Token holders can have voting rights, access to exclusive content, and opportunities to collaborate with the author.
5. **Decentralized Publishing Platforms**: Emerging decentralized publishing platforms leverage blockchain technology to provide authors with more control over their work and revenue. These platforms eliminate traditional gatekeepers, allowing authors to publish and distribute their work directly to readers.

Case Study: Experimenting with Innovative Revenue Models

An author decides to experiment with a subscription-based revenue model using NFTs. They create a series of NFTs that grant subscribers access to exclusive monthly content, including new chapters, behind-the-scenes insights, and interactive events.

Subscribers purchase the NFTs, which automatically renew each month through a smart contract. The author benefits from a steady stream of revenue and a dedicated subscriber base. The subscription model allows the author to engage with their readers on an ongoing basis, providing fresh and exclusive content that keeps subscribers excited and invested.

The future opportunities for authors in the NFT and blockchain space are vast and varied. By staying informed about emerging trends and technologies, authors can experiment with innovative revenue models, collaborative projects, interactive storytelling, and tokenized communities. Embracing these opportunities can help authors remain competitive, engage with their audience in new ways, and maximize the potential of their creative works. As the digital landscape continues to evolve, authors who leverage NFTs and blockchain technology will be well-positioned to thrive in the future of digital publishing.

Section Two
Best Practices for Authors Using NFTs and Blockchain

11. Ownership and Intellectual Property Rights 43
12. Authenticity and Verification 46
13. Platform Selection 48
14. Metadata and Additional Content 50
15. Licensing and Usage Rights 53
16. Pricing and Revenue Models 56
17. Promotion and Marketing 59
18. Community Engagement 62
19. Legal and Tax Implications 64
20. Continuous Learning and Adaptation 67

11
Ownership and Intellectual Property Rights

As authors venture into the world of NFTs and blockchain, it's essential to ensure that they have the legal rights to tokenize and sell their works. Verifying ownership and clearing any copyright or licensing issues is crucial to protect their intellectual property. This chapter explores best practices for authors to safeguard their rights and navigate the legal complexities of NFTs and blockchain.

Ensuring Legal Ownership and Rights

Before tokenizing their works as NFTs, authors must ensure that they have the necessary legal rights to do so. This involves verifying ownership, clearing any copyright or licensing issues, and understanding the legal implications of tokenizing and selling their work on the blockchain.

Best Practices for Protecting Intellectual Property

1. **Copyright Registration**: Authors should register their works with the appropriate copyright office to establish legal ownership. Copyright registration provides a formal record of ownership and strengthens the author's legal position in case of disputes.
2. **Clearance of Rights**: Authors must ensure that they have cleared all necessary rights before tokenizing their works. This includes obtaining permissions for any third-party content, such as images, music, or text, used in their work.

3. **Legal Agreements**: Authors should consider using legal agreements to define the terms of use for their NFTs. These agreements can specify the rights granted to the NFT holder, such as display, reproduction, and resale rights, and ensure that the author's intentions are clearly communicated.
4. **Consultation with Legal Professionals**: Navigating the legal complexities of NFTs and blockchain can be challenging. Authors should consult with legal professionals who specialize in intellectual property and blockchain technology to ensure compliance with relevant laws and regulations.

Case Study: Protecting Intellectual Property with Copyright Registration

An author decides to tokenize their electronic book as an NFT. Before doing so, they register the book with the copyright office, establishing a formal record of ownership. The author also obtains permissions for any third-party content used in the book and consults with a legal professional to draft a legal agreement specifying the terms of use for the NFT.

By taking these steps, the author ensures that their intellectual property is protected and that they have the legal rights to tokenize and sell their work as an NFT. The formal record of ownership and the legal agreement provide a strong legal foundation in case of any disputes.

Ensuring legal ownership and protecting intellectual property rights are crucial steps for authors venturing into the world of NFTs and blockchain. By following best practices such as copyright registration, clearance of rights, legal agreements, and consultation with legal professionals, authors can safeguard their rights and navigate the legal complexities of tokenizing and selling their work. Embracing these best practices can help authors protect their intellectual property and thrive in the digital publishing landscape.

12
Authenticity and Verification

Establishing the authenticity of NFTs is essential for authors to build trust with their readers and protect their work from plagiarism and counterfeiting. By providing unique and verifiable metadata, authors can ensure the credibility of their NFTs and guard against unauthorized copying. This chapter explores best practices for establishing authenticity and verification for NFTs.

Establishing Authenticity with Verifiable Metadata

Metadata plays a crucial role in establishing the authenticity of NFTs. By including detailed and verifiable metadata, authors can provide important information about their work, its creation process, and associated rights. This metadata serves as a digital certificate of authenticity, ensuring that the NFT is genuine and credible.

Best Practices for Authenticity and Verification

1. **Detailed Descriptions**: Authors should include detailed descriptions of their work in the metadata, such as the title, creation date, and a summary of the content. This information helps verify the authenticity of the NFT and provides context for potential buyers.
2. **Creation Process Information**: Including information about the creation process, such as the tools and techniques used, adds credibility to the NFT. Authors can also include digital signatures or certificates from trusted sources to further verify the authenticity of their work.
3. **Associated Rights**: Authors should clearly specify the rights associated with the NFT in the metadata. This

includes information about display, reproduction, and resale rights, ensuring that buyers understand the terms of use and the author's intentions.

4. **Unique Identifiers**: Each NFT should have a unique identifier that distinguishes it from other tokens. This identifier can be a digital watermark, QR code, or other unique markers that ensure the NFT is genuine and cannot be replicated.

Case Study: Verifying Authenticity with Detailed Metadata

An author decides to tokenize their electronic book as an NFT. They include detailed metadata for the NFT, such as the book's title, creation date, and a summary of the content. The author also provides information about the creation process, including the writing tools and software used.

To further verify the authenticity of the NFT, the author includes a digital signature and a certificate of authenticity from a trusted literary organization. The metadata also specifies the associated rights, such as display and resale rights, ensuring that buyers understand the terms of use.

By providing detailed and verifiable metadata, the author ensures that the NFT is genuine and credible. Potential buyers can trust that they are purchasing an authentic and unique digital copy of the electronic book.

Establishing authenticity and verification for NFTs is essential for building trust and protecting intellectual property. By providing detailed and verifiable metadata, including information about the creation process, associated rights, and unique identifiers, authors can ensure the credibility of their NFTs and guard against unauthorized copying. Embracing these best practices can help authors establish trust with their readers and thrive in the digital publishing landscape.

13
Platform Selection

Choosing the right NFT marketplace or platform is crucial for authors to successfully mint and sell their NFTs. Factors such as reputation, user base, transaction fees, ease of use, and community engagement play a significant role in selecting a platform that aligns with the author's goals and target audience. This chapter explores best practices for selecting the right platform for minting and selling NFTs.

Factors to Consider When Choosing an NFT Platform

1. **Reputation**: Authors should research the reputation of the NFT platform to ensure it is trustworthy and reliable. Reading reviews, checking user feedback, and exploring the platform's track record can provide valuable insights into its credibility.
2. **User Base**: The size and demographics of the platform's user base are important considerations. Authors should choose a platform with a large and active user base that aligns with their target audience, increasing the likelihood of attracting potential buyers.
3. **Transaction Fees**: Different NFT platforms charge varying transaction fees for minting and selling NFTs. Authors should compare the fees and understand the cost structure to ensure it aligns with their budget and revenue goals.
4. **Ease of Use**: The platform's user interface and ease of use are critical factors. Authors should select a platform that is user-friendly and provides clear instructions for

minting and selling NFTs, making the process as seamless as possible.

5. **Community Engagement**: A strong and engaged community can significantly impact the success of an NFT. Authors should choose a platform that fosters community engagement, providing opportunities for interaction, promotion, and support.

Case Study: Selecting the Right NFT Platform

An author is looking to mint and sell their electronic book as an NFT. They research various NFT platforms, comparing factors such as reputation, user base, transaction fees, ease of use, and community engagement.

After careful consideration, the author selects a reputable platform with a large and active user base that aligns with their target audience. The platform has reasonable transaction fees and a user-friendly interface, making it easy for the author to mint and sell their NFT. Additionally, the platform fosters a strong community, providing opportunities for the author to promote their work and engage with potential buyers.

By selecting the right platform, the author successfully mints and sells their NFT, reaching a wide audience and generating significant revenue from their electronic book.

Choosing the right NFT platform is crucial for the success of minting and selling NFTs. By considering factors such as reputation, user base, transaction fees, ease of use, and community engagement, authors can select a platform that aligns with their goals and target audience. Embracing these best practices can help authors successfully navigate the NFT marketplace and maximize the potential of their creative works.

14
Metadata and Additional Content

Metadata and additional content play a vital role in enhancing the value and appeal of NFTs. By enriching their NFTs with meaningful metadata and supplementary content, authors can provide a richer and more engaging experience for collectors. This chapter explores best practices for curating metadata and additional content for NFTs.

Enhancing NFTs with Metadata and Additional Content

Metadata provides essential information about an NFT, while additional content adds value and enhances the collector's experience. Authors can use metadata to describe their work, provide context, and establish authenticity, while additional content can include supplementary materials, multimedia elements, and exclusive features.

Best Practices for Metadata and Additional Content

1. **Detailed Metadata**: Authors should provide detailed metadata for their NFTs, including information such as the title, creation date, description, and creator's information. This metadata helps verify the authenticity of the NFT and provides context for potential buyers.
2. **Supplementary Content**: Authors can enhance their NFTs with supplementary content, such as behind-the-scenes insights, making-of videos, and exclusive interviews. This additional content adds value and provides a richer experience for collectors.
3. **Multimedia Elements**: Incorporating multimedia elements such as images, audio clips, and videos can

make the NFT more engaging and interactive. Authors can use these elements to enhance the storytelling experience and provide unique and immersive content.
4. **Exclusive Features**: Offering exclusive features, such as access to private events, early access to new releases, and special merchandise, can increase the appeal of the NFT. These features reward collectors and create a sense of exclusivity.

Case Study: Enriching an NFT with Metadata and Additional Content

An author decides to tokenize their electronic book as an NFT and enrich it with detailed metadata and additional content. The metadata includes the book's title, creation date, a detailed description, and the author's information. The author also provides supplementary content, such as behind-the-scenes videos of the writing process, an exclusive interview with the author, and high-resolution images of the book's cover art.

To further enhance the NFT, the author incorporates multimedia elements, including audio clips of selected chapters and a video tour of the book's setting. The NFT also grants access to a private online event where the author discusses the book and answers questions from collectors.

By providing detailed metadata and enriching the NFT with additional content, the author creates a valuable and engaging digital collectible that attracts collectors and enhances the overall experience.

Enriching NFTs with detailed metadata and additional content is essential for enhancing their value and appeal. By providing comprehensive information, supplementary materials, multimedia elements, and exclusive features, authors can create engaging and valuable digital collectibles that attract collectors and provide a richer experience. Embracing these best practices can help authors maximize the potential of their NFTs and build a loyal and engaged audience.

15
Licensing and Usage Rights

When creating and selling NFTs, it is crucial for authors to clearly define the licensing terms and usage rights associated with their digital assets. Clear communication of these terms helps manage expectations and avoid potential conflicts. This chapter explores best practices for defining and communicating licensing and usage rights for NFTs.

Defining Licensing and Usage Rights

Licensing terms and usage rights specify what the NFT holder can and cannot do with the digital asset. Authors must clearly define these terms to ensure that buyers understand the scope of their rights and obligations.

Best Practices for Licensing and Usage Rights

1. **Clear Definitions**: Authors should provide clear definitions of the licensing terms and usage rights associated with their NFTs. This includes specifying whether the NFT grants the purchaser the right to display, reproduce, resell, or access additional content related to the work.
2. **Detailed Agreements**: Authors should create detailed licensing agreements that outline the specific rights and limitations associated with the NFT. These agreements should be easily accessible to buyers and written in clear, understandable language.
3. **Usage Limitations**: Authors should specify any usage limitations in the licensing agreement. This includes restrictions on commercial use, modifications, and redistribution of the digital asset. Clearly defining these

limitations helps prevent unauthorized use and protects the author's rights.

4. **Rights Retention**: Authors should retain certain rights to their work, even after selling the NFT. This includes the right to create derivative works, use the content for promotional purposes, and retain ownership of the original intellectual property.
5. **Consultation with Legal Professionals**: To ensure that the licensing terms and usage rights are legally sound and enforceable, authors should consult with legal professionals who specialize in intellectual property and blockchain technology.

Case Study: Defining Licensing Terms for an NFT

An author decides to tokenize their electronic book as an NFT and create a detailed licensing agreement to define the usage rights. The agreement specifies that the NFT holder has the right to display and resell the digital copy of the book but cannot reproduce, modify, or distribute it for commercial purposes.

The author also retains the rights to create derivative works, use the content for promotional purposes, and maintain ownership of the original intellectual property. The licensing agreement is written in clear, understandable language and is accessible to buyers through the NFT platform.

By providing clear definitions and detailed agreements, the author ensures that buyers understand the scope of their rights and obligations. This helps manage expectations, prevent unauthorized use, and protect the author's rights.

Defining and communicating licensing and usage rights is essential for authors creating and selling NFTs. By providing clear definitions, detailed agreements, and specifying usage limitations, authors can ensure that buyers understand their rights and obligations. Consulting with legal professionals can help authors create legally sound and enforceable licensing terms. Embracing these best practices can help authors protect their rights and maximize the potential of their NFTs.

16
Pricing and Revenue Models

Determining the pricing strategy and revenue model for NFTs is a critical step for authors looking to maximize their earnings. Various factors, including the uniqueness of the work, market demand, and the author's objectives, influence pricing decisions. This chapter explores best practices for setting prices and choosing revenue models for NFTs.

Setting Prices for NFTs

1. **Market Research**: Authors should conduct market research to understand the pricing trends for similar NFTs. Analyzing the prices of comparable digital assets can provide insights into what buyers are willing to pay.
2. **Perceived Value**: The perceived value of the NFT plays a significant role in pricing. Authors should consider factors such as the uniqueness of the work, the quality of the content, and any additional features or exclusivity that add value.
3. **Tiered Pricing**: Authors can experiment with tiered pricing models, offering different levels of access or exclusivity at varying price points. This approach caters to different segments of the market and maximizes revenue potential.
4. **Auctions**: Auctions can be an effective way to determine the market value of an NFT. By allowing buyers to bid on the NFT, authors can achieve higher prices and create a sense of competition and urgency.

Choosing Revenue Models

1. **Fixed Pricing**: Fixed pricing involves setting a predetermined price for the NFT. This approach provides clarity and simplicity for buyers and can be effective for works with established value.
2. **Auctions**: Auctions allow buyers to bid on the NFT, with the highest bidder winning the asset. This model can drive higher prices and is suitable for unique or highly sought-after works.
3. **Tiered Offerings**: Tiered offerings provide different levels of access or exclusivity at varying price points. For example, an author can offer standard editions, limited editions, and exclusive editions of their work, each with different features and pricing.
4. **Royalties from Secondary Sales**: Authors can earn ongoing revenue by receiving royalties from secondary market sales. Smart contracts can be programmed to automatically distribute a percentage of the resale value to the original author, providing continuous income.

Case Study: Implementing a Tiered Pricing Model

An author decides to tokenize their electronic book as an NFT and implement a tiered pricing model. They create three tiers: a standard edition, a limited edition with exclusive illustrations, and a collector's edition with additional content and access to a private event.

The standard edition is priced at a fixed amount, the limited edition is offered at a higher price, and the collector's edition is auctioned to the highest bidder. The author also programs a smart contract to receive royalties from any secondary sales of the NFTs.

By implementing a tiered pricing model, the author caters to different segments of the market and maximizes revenue potential. The auction for the collector's edition generates significant interest and achieves a high price, while the royalties from secondary sales provide ongoing income.

Setting prices and choosing revenue models for NFTs requires careful consideration of market trends, perceived value, and the author's objectives. By conducting market research, considering perceived value, experimenting with tiered pricing, and exploring different revenue models, authors can maximize their earnings and reach a wider audience. Embracing these best practices can help authors navigate the NFT marketplace and achieve financial success with their digital assets.

17
Promotion and Marketing

Creating NFTs is only the first step; actively promoting and marketing them is crucial for success. Authors need to build awareness, communicate with potential buyers, and foster a supportive community around their NFTs. This chapter explores best practices for promoting and marketing NFTs.

Effective Promotion and Marketing Strategies

1. **Social Media**: Leveraging social media platforms is essential for promoting NFTs. Authors should use platforms like Twitter, Instagram, and Facebook to share updates, engage with followers, and build excitement around their NFTs.
2. **Online Forums and Communities**: Participating in online forums and communities dedicated to NFTs and blockchain technology can help authors connect with potential buyers and collectors. Engaging in discussions, sharing insights, and showcasing NFTs can generate interest and support.
3. **Email Newsletters**: Building an email list and sending regular newsletters is an effective way to keep followers informed about new NFT releases, exclusive offers, and upcoming events. Email marketing can help maintain a direct connection with potential buyers.
4. **Collaborations**: Collaborating with other authors, artists, and influencers can expand reach and attract new audiences. Joint promotions, cross-promotions, and co-created content can generate buzz and increase visibility.
5. **Content Marketing**: Creating and sharing valuable content related to NFTs and blockchain technology can

position authors as thought leaders in the space. Blog posts, articles, and videos can educate potential buyers and build credibility.

Case Study: Promoting an NFT Release

An author is preparing to release their electronic book as an NFT. They develop a comprehensive promotion and marketing strategy, leveraging social media, online forums, email newsletters, collaborations, and content marketing.

The author starts by announcing the upcoming NFT release on social media, sharing teasers and behind-the-scenes content to build anticipation. They engage with followers, respond to questions, and create interactive posts to generate excitement.

Simultaneously, the author participates in online forums and communities dedicated to NFTs, sharing insights and showcasing the unique features of their NFT. They also collaborate with a well-known influencer in the NFT space, who promotes the release to their followers.

The author sends an email newsletter to their subscriber list, providing exclusive details about the NFT release and offering early access to loyal followers. Additionally, they publish a series of blog posts and videos explaining the benefits of NFTs and blockchain technology, positioning themselves as a knowledgeable and credible source.

The comprehensive promotion and marketing strategy generates significant interest and excitement, leading to a successful NFT release. The author attracts a wide audience, achieves strong sales, and builds a supportive community around their NFTs.

Effective promotion and marketing are essential for the success of NFTs. By leveraging social media, online forums, email newsletters, collaborations, and content marketing, authors can build awareness, engage with potential buyers, and foster a supportive community. Embracing these best practices can help authors successfully promote and market their NFTs, maximizing their reach and potential earnings.

18
Community Engagement

Building a strong and supportive community is crucial for the long-term success of NFTs. Engaging with collectors, fans, and the NFT community can generate interest, loyalty, and support. This chapter explores best practices for actively engaging with the NFT community.

Strategies for Community Engagement

1. **Active Communication**: Authors should actively communicate with their community through social media, online forums, and other platforms. Responding to questions, sharing updates, and engaging in discussions can build trust and foster a sense of connection.
2. **Exclusive Content**: Offering exclusive content and experiences to the community can reward loyalty and generate excitement. This can include early access to new releases, behind-the-scenes content, and special events.
3. **Interactive Events**: Hosting interactive events such as Q&A sessions, virtual meet-and-greets, and live streams can engage the community and provide unique opportunities for interaction. These events can help build a strong sense of community and loyalty.
4. **Collaborations and Partnerships**: Collaborating with other creators, artists, and influencers in the NFT space can expand reach and attract new members to the community. Joint projects and cross-promotions can create a sense of excitement and support.
5. **Feedback and Improvement**: Actively seeking feedback from the community and making improvements based on

their input can enhance the overall experience. Listening to the community and addressing their needs can build trust and loyalty.

Case Study: Building a Supportive NFT Community

An author decides to build a strong and supportive community around their NFTs. They start by actively communicating with their followers on social media, responding to questions, and sharing regular updates about their work and upcoming releases.

To reward loyalty, the author offers exclusive content to the community, including early access to new NFT releases, behind-the-scenes insights, and special merchandise. They also host interactive events such as virtual meet-and-greets and live Q&A sessions, providing unique opportunities for interaction.

The author collaborates with other creators and influencers in the NFT space, working on joint projects and promoting each other's work. These collaborations generate excitement and attract new members to the community.

To ensure continuous improvement, the author actively seeks feedback from the community, asking for suggestions and making changes based on their input. This approach builds trust and loyalty, creating a supportive and engaged community around the author's NFTs.

Community engagement is essential for the long-term success of NFTs. By actively communicating with the community, offering exclusive content, hosting interactive events, collaborating with others, and seeking feedback, authors can build a strong and supportive community. Embracing these best practices can help authors generate interest, loyalty, and support for their NFTs, ensuring ongoing success in the digital space.

19
Legal and Tax Implications

Creating and selling NFTs involves various legal and tax implications that authors must be aware of. Understanding and complying with relevant regulations is crucial to avoid potential legal issues and ensure proper handling of tax obligations. This chapter explores best practices for navigating the legal and tax implications of NFTs.

Understanding Legal and Tax Implications

1. **Intellectual Property Rights**: Authors must ensure they have the legal rights to tokenize and sell their work as NFTs. This includes verifying ownership, clearing any copyright or licensing issues, and understanding the legal implications of tokenizing intellectual property.
2. **Smart Contracts**: Smart contracts used in NFTs must comply with legal standards and regulations. Authors should ensure that the terms and conditions outlined in the smart contract are legally enforceable and protect their rights.
3. **Tax Obligations**: Selling NFTs may have tax implications, including income tax, capital gains tax, and sales tax. Authors must understand their tax obligations and ensure proper reporting and payment of taxes related to NFT transactions.

Best Practices for Navigating Legal and Tax Implications

1. **Consult with Legal Professionals**: Authors should consult with legal professionals who specialize in

intellectual property and blockchain technology. Legal experts can provide guidance on copyright, licensing, and compliance with relevant regulations.

2. **Seek Tax Advice**: Authors should seek advice from tax professionals to understand their tax obligations related to NFT transactions. Tax experts can provide guidance on reporting income, calculating capital gains, and ensuring compliance with tax regulations.
3. **Clear Licensing Agreements**: Authors should create clear and detailed licensing agreements that outline the terms and conditions of the NFT sale. These agreements should specify the rights granted to the NFT holder, usage limitations, and any royalties or revenue-sharing arrangements.
4. **Accurate Record-Keeping**: Keeping accurate records of NFT transactions is essential for legal and tax compliance. Authors should maintain detailed records of sales, income, expenses, and royalties to ensure proper reporting and compliance.

Case Study: Navigating Legal and Tax Implications

An author decides to tokenize their electronic book as an NFT. Before proceeding, they consult with a legal professional to ensure they have the necessary rights to tokenize and sell their work. The legal professional helps the author create a clear licensing agreement that outlines the terms and conditions of the NFT sale.

The author also seeks advice from a tax professional to understand their tax obligations related to NFT transactions. The tax professional provides guidance on reporting income, calculating capital gains, and ensuring compliance with tax regulations.

By consulting with legal and tax professionals, the author ensures they navigate the legal and tax implications of NFTs correctly. They create clear licensing agreements, maintain accurate records, and comply with relevant regulations, avoiding potential legal issues and ensuring proper handling of tax obligations.

Navigating the legal and tax implications of NFTs is crucial for authors to avoid potential legal issues and ensure proper handling of tax obligations. By consulting with legal and tax professionals, creating clear licensing agreements, and maintaining accurate records, authors can ensure compliance with relevant regulations and protect their rights. Embracing these best practices can help authors navigate the complexities of NFTs and achieve success in the digital space.

20
Continuous Learning and Adaptation

The NFT space is constantly evolving, with new trends, technologies, and market developments emerging regularly. For authors to stay competitive and seize new opportunities, continuous learning and adaptation are essential. This chapter explores best practices for staying informed and adapting to changes in the NFT space.

Embracing Continuous Learning

1. **Stay Informed**: Authors should stay informed about the latest trends, technologies, and market developments in the NFT space. Following industry news, reading articles, and participating in online forums can provide valuable insights.
2. **Attend Events and Webinars**: Attending industry events, conferences, and webinars can help authors learn from experts, network with peers, and stay up-to-date with the latest developments. These events provide opportunities for learning and growth.
3. **Engage with the Community**: Engaging with the NFT community can provide valuable insights and feedback. Authors should participate in discussions, ask questions, and learn from the experiences of others in the community.
4. **Experiment and Innovate**: Authors should be open to experimenting with new ideas and innovating in their approach to NFTs. Trying new strategies, exploring different revenue models, and adapting to changing market conditions can help authors stay competitive.

Best Practices for Continuous Learning and Adaptation

1. **Set Learning Goals**: Authors should set specific learning goals to stay focused and motivated. This can include learning about new technologies, understanding market trends, or improving skills related to NFTs and blockchain.
2. **Create a Learning Plan**: Developing a learning plan can help authors stay organized and track their progress. The plan should outline the resources, events, and activities that will help achieve their learning goals.
3. **Seek Mentorship and Guidance**: Finding mentors or seeking guidance from experienced individuals in the NFT space can provide valuable insights and support. Mentors can offer advice, share experiences, and help authors navigate challenges.
4. **Adapt to Changes**: Authors should be flexible and willing to adapt to changes in the NFT space. This includes staying open to new ideas, learning from failures, and continuously improving their approach.

Case Study: Embracing Continuous Learning and Adaptation

An author decides to embrace continuous learning and adaptation to stay competitive in the NFT space. They set specific learning goals, such as understanding new blockchain technologies and exploring innovative revenue models.

The author creates a learning plan that includes attending industry conferences, participating in webinars, and reading articles about the latest trends. They also engage with the NFT community, participating in online discussions and seeking feedback from peers.

To stay flexible and adapt to changes, the author experiments with different strategies and revenue models, learning from their successes and failures. They seek guidance from mentors who provide valuable insights and support.

By embracing continuous learning and adaptation, the author stays informed about the latest developments, improves their skills, and remains competitive in the NFT space. This approach helps them seize new opportunities and achieve long-term success.

Continuous learning and adaptation are essential for authors to stay competitive and seize new opportunities in the NFT space. By setting learning goals, creating a learning plan, seeking mentorship, and adapting to changes, authors can stay informed and continuously improve their approach. Embracing these best practices can help authors navigate the evolving NFT landscape and achieve success in the digital space.

Section Three
Technical and Legal Considerations

33. Understanding Blockchain Technology 71
34. Authenticity and Copyright 74
35. Tokenization 77
36. Privacy and Confidentiality 80
37. Distribution and Access 83
38. Royalty Tracking and Payments 86
39. Scalability and Transaction Costs 89
40. Backup and Recovery 92
41. User Experience 95
42. Legal and Regulatory Considerations 98
43. Continuous Learning and Adaptation 101
44. Future Opportunities 104

21
Understanding Blockchain Technology

Authors should have a solid understanding of blockchain technology, including its decentralized nature, immutability, and transparency. Familiarizing themselves with the basics of blockchain will help authors make informed decisions and leverage the technology effectively.

Understanding Blockchain Technology

1. **Decentralization**: Blockchain operates on a decentralized network of nodes, which means no single entity has control over the entire network. This decentralization ensures security, transparency, and resistance to censorship.
2. **Immutability**: Once data is recorded on the blockchain, it cannot be altered or deleted. This immutability ensures a permanent and tamper-proof record of transactions, providing trust and accountability.
3. **Transparency**: Blockchain transactions are publicly recorded and can be verified by anyone. This transparency enhances trust and allows for the verification of ownership and transaction history.

Best Practices for Understanding Blockchain Technology

1. **Learn the Basics**: Authors should start by learning the basics of blockchain technology, including how it works, its key features, and its potential applications. Online courses, tutorials, and articles can provide a solid foundation.

2. **Explore Use Cases**: Understanding real-world use cases of blockchain technology can provide valuable insights into its potential. Authors can explore how blockchain is used in various industries, including digital publishing, finance, and supply chain management.
3. **Stay Updated**: Blockchain technology is constantly evolving, with new developments and innovations emerging regularly. Authors should stay updated on the latest trends and advancements to understand the technology's potential and limitations.
4. **Engage with Experts**: Engaging with blockchain experts and communities can provide valuable insights and guidance. Authors can participate in forums, attend conferences, and seek mentorship to deepen their understanding.

Case Study: Learning About Blockchain Technology

An author decides to learn about blockchain technology to leverage its potential for their NFTs. They start by taking an online course on blockchain basics, gaining an understanding of how the technology works and its key features.

The author explores real-world use cases of blockchain, learning how it is used in digital publishing, finance, and other industries. They stay updated on the latest developments by following industry news and participating in online forums.

To deepen their understanding, the author engages with blockchain experts and seeks guidance from mentors. This approach helps the author make informed decisions and effectively leverage blockchain technology for their NFTs.

Understanding blockchain technology is essential for authors looking to leverage its potential for their NFTs. By learning the basics, exploring use cases, staying updated, and engaging with experts, authors can make informed decisions and effectively utilize blockchain technology. Embracing these best practices can help authors navigate the complexities of blockchain and achieve success in the digital space.

22
Authenticity and Copyright

Blockchain can provide a unique digital signature that ensures the originality and authenticity of electronic books. Authors should be diligent in verifying ownership and ensuring they have the necessary rights to publish their works on the blockchain. Clearing any copyright or licensing issues is crucial to protect their intellectual property.

Ensuring Authenticity and Copyright Protection

1. **Unique Digital Signatures**: Blockchain technology can create a unique digital signature for each electronic book, ensuring its authenticity and originality. This digital signature acts as a proof of ownership and can be used to verify the work's authenticity.
2. **Verification of Ownership**: Authors must verify their ownership and ensure they have the necessary rights to publish their works on the blockchain. This includes clearing any copyright or licensing issues and obtaining permissions for third-party content.
3. **Digital Rights Management**: Authors can use blockchain technology to manage digital rights and enforce usage limitations. Smart contracts can specify the terms of use, ensuring the content remains protected and used in accordance with the author's intentions.

Best Practices for Authenticity and Copyright Protection

1. **Clear Ownership and Rights**: Authors should ensure they have clear ownership and the necessary rights to tokenize and sell their work as NFTs. This includes

verifying ownership, clearing copyright issues, and obtaining permissions for third-party content.

2. **Unique Metadata**: Including unique metadata in the NFT, such as the title, creation date, and creator's information, helps verify the work's authenticity and provides context for potential buyers.
3. **Smart Contracts**: Using smart contracts to define and enforce usage rights can help protect the author's work. Smart contracts can specify usage limitations, royalties, and other terms, ensuring the content is used in accordance with the author's intentions.
4. **Legal Consultation**: Consulting with legal professionals who specialize in intellectual property and blockchain technology can help authors navigate copyright and licensing issues. Legal experts can provide guidance on protecting intellectual property and ensuring compliance with relevant regulations.

Case Study: Protecting Intellectual Property with Blockchain

An author decides to tokenize their electronic book as an NFT and use blockchain technology to ensure its authenticity and protect their copyright. They verify their ownership and clear any copyright issues, obtaining permissions for third-party content used in the book.

The author includes unique metadata in the NFT, such as the title, creation date, and creator's information, to verify the work's authenticity. They use a smart contract to define the usage rights, specifying limitations on reproduction, distribution, and modification.

By consulting with a legal professional, the author ensures that their intellectual property is protected and that they comply with relevant regulations. This approach helps the author safeguard their work and maintain control over its usage.

NFT and Blockchain Essentials

Ensuring authenticity and protecting copyright are crucial for authors using blockchain technology. By verifying ownership, including unique metadata, using smart contracts, and consulting with legal professionals, authors can safeguard their intellectual property and ensure compliance with relevant regulations. Embracing these best practices can help authors protect their work and thrive in the digital space.

23
Tokenization

Authors can consider tokenizing their electronic books as Non-Fungible Tokens (NFTs) on the blockchain. Tokenization enables the creation of unique digital assets that can represent ownership or access to specific electronic books. Authors should understand the tokenization process and the benefits it offers in terms of proof of ownership and verifiability.

Understanding the Tokenization Process

1. **Creating the NFT**: The tokenization process involves creating a unique digital token on the blockchain that represents the electronic book. This token includes metadata that provides information about the book, such as the title, author, creation date, and a description.
2. **Smart Contracts**: Smart contracts are used to define the terms and conditions associated with the NFT. This includes specifying usage rights, royalties, and any other terms that govern the NFT's use and ownership.
3. **Minting the NFT**: Minting involves creating the NFT on the blockchain, which includes recording the metadata and smart contract details. This process makes the NFT available for purchase and transfer on the blockchain.

Benefits of Tokenization

1. **Proof of Ownership**: Tokenization provides a verifiable proof of ownership for the electronic book. The blockchain ledger records all transactions, creating a transparent and tamper-proof history of ownership.

2. **Verifiability**: The unique digital signature of the NFT ensures the authenticity and originality of the electronic book. Buyers can verify the authenticity of the NFT by checking the blockchain ledger.
3. **Enhanced Control**: Tokenization allows authors to retain control over the distribution and use of their work. Smart contracts can enforce usage rights and ensure that the content is used in accordance with the author's intentions.
4. **Revenue Opportunities**: Tokenization creates new revenue opportunities for authors. In addition to selling the NFT, authors can earn royalties from secondary market sales and offer exclusive content or features to NFT holders.

Case Study: Tokenizing an Electronic Book

An author decides to tokenize their electronic book as an NFT. They create the NFT on a blockchain platform, including metadata that provides information about the book, such as the title, author, creation date, and a description.

The author uses a smart contract to define the usage rights, specifying that the NFT holder has the right to display and resell the digital copy of the book but cannot reproduce or modify it for commercial purposes. The smart contract also includes a royalty clause, ensuring that the author receives a percentage of any secondary market sales.

The author mints the NFT on the blockchain, making it available for purchase and transfer. By tokenizing their electronic book, the author provides a verifiable proof of ownership, ensures the authenticity of the work, and creates new revenue opportunities through sales and royalties.

Tokenizing electronic books as NFTs provides authors with a powerful tool to create unique digital assets that represent ownership and access. By understanding the tokenization process and leveraging the benefits of proof of ownership, verifiability, enhanced control, and revenue opportunities, authors can maximize the potential of their digital works. Embracing these best practices can help authors successfully tokenize their electronic books and thrive in the digital space.

24
Privacy and Confidentiality

Authors should be mindful of the privacy and confidentiality implications when using blockchain. Depending on the blockchain network chosen, some information may be visible to the public. Authors should assess the sensitivity of their content and evaluate whether private or permissioned blockchains are more suitable for their needs.

Understanding Privacy and Confidentiality

1. **Public vs. Private Blockchains**: Public blockchains are open to anyone and provide full transparency, while private blockchains restrict access to authorized participants. Authors should consider the level of privacy and confidentiality required for their work when choosing a blockchain network.
2. **Data Sensitivity**: Authors should assess the sensitivity of the content they plan to tokenize. If the content includes sensitive information or proprietary data, a private or permissioned blockchain may be more appropriate to ensure confidentiality.
3. **Data Encryption**: Encrypting data before recording it on the blockchain can enhance privacy and protect sensitive information. Authors should consider using encryption techniques to safeguard their content.

Best Practices for Privacy and Confidentiality

1. **Choose the Right Blockchain**: Authors should choose a blockchain network that aligns with their privacy and confidentiality needs. Public blockchains offer

transparency, while private or permissioned blockchains provide greater control over access and data visibility.

2. **Assess Data Sensitivity**: Authors should assess the sensitivity of their content and determine whether it includes proprietary information, personal data, or other sensitive details. This assessment will guide the choice of blockchain and the level of privacy required.
3. **Use Data Encryption**: Encrypting data before recording it on the blockchain can enhance privacy and protect sensitive information. Authors should consider using encryption techniques to ensure the confidentiality of their content.
4. **Consult with Experts**: Consulting with blockchain and data privacy experts can provide valuable insights and guidance. Experts can help authors navigate privacy and confidentiality challenges and ensure compliance with relevant regulations.

Case Study: Ensuring Privacy and Confidentiality for an NFT

An author decides to tokenize their electronic book as an NFT but is concerned about the privacy and confidentiality of the content. The book includes proprietary information that the author wants to protect.

To address these concerns, the author chooses a permissioned blockchain that restricts access to authorized participants. They also use data encryption techniques to safeguard the content before recording it on the blockchain.

By consulting with blockchain and data privacy experts, the author ensures that the content is protected and that the privacy and confidentiality requirements are met. This approach helps the author maintain control over the sensitive information while leveraging the benefits of blockchain technology.

NFT and Blockchain Essentials

Privacy and confidentiality are crucial considerations for authors using blockchain technology. By choosing the right blockchain network, assessing data sensitivity, using data encryption, and consulting with experts, authors can protect their content and ensure confidentiality. Embracing these best practices can help authors navigate privacy challenges and successfully tokenize their electronic works in the digital space.

25
Distribution and Access

Blockchain technology enables easy and secure distribution of electronic books. Authors should explore blockchain-based platforms or marketplaces that provide a user-friendly interface for readers to access their works. It's essential to consider factors such as user base, ease of use, and discoverability when selecting a platform.

Leveraging Blockchain for Distribution and Access

1. **Blockchain-Based Platforms**: Authors can distribute their electronic books through blockchain-based platforms or marketplaces that offer secure and transparent transactions. These platforms provide a user-friendly interface for readers to access and purchase NFTs.
2. **User Experience**: The user experience is a critical factor in the success of NFT distribution. Authors should choose platforms that offer a seamless and intuitive experience for readers, making it easy to browse, purchase, and access electronic books.
3. **Discoverability**: Increasing the discoverability of NFTs is essential for reaching a wider audience. Authors should select platforms that offer robust search and discovery features, helping readers find their works easily.

Best Practices for Distribution and Access

1. **Choose the Right Platform**: Authors should research and choose blockchain-based platforms that align with their goals and target audience. Factors such as user

base, ease of use, transaction fees, and discoverability should be considered.
2. **Optimize User Experience**: Ensuring a positive user experience is crucial for attracting and retaining readers. Authors should choose platforms that offer a seamless and intuitive interface, making it easy for readers to access and purchase their NFTs.
3. **Enhance Discoverability**: Increasing the discoverability of NFTs can help authors reach a wider audience. Authors should use tags, keywords, and categories to make their works more searchable and visible on the platform.
4. **Engage with Readers**: Engaging with readers through the platform can enhance the distribution and access experience. Authors should respond to questions, participate in discussions, and provide updates to keep readers informed and engaged.

Case Study: Distributing an NFT through a Blockchain-Based Platform

An author decides to distribute their electronic book as an NFT through a blockchain-based platform. They research various platforms and choose one with a large and active user base, a user-friendly interface, and robust search and discovery features.

To optimize the user experience, the author ensures that the metadata and additional content are clear and comprehensive. They use relevant tags and keywords to increase the discoverability of their NFT on the platform.

The author actively engages with readers through the platform, responding to questions, sharing updates, and participating in discussions. This approach enhances the distribution and access experience, attracting a wider audience and increasing sales.

Leveraging blockchain technology for the distribution and access of electronic books offers authors a secure and transparent way to reach their audience. By choosing the right platform, optimizing user experience, enhancing discoverability, and engaging with readers, authors can successfully distribute their NFTs and maximize their reach. Embracing these best practices can help authors thrive in the digital space and connect with readers worldwide.

26
Royalty Tracking and Payments

Smart contracts on the blockchain can automate royalty tracking and distribution. Authors should leverage this feature to ensure transparent and instant payments whenever their electronic books are sold or accessed. Understanding how smart contracts work and customizing them to suit their specific royalty requirements is crucial.

Leveraging Smart Contracts for Royalty Tracking

1. **Automated Royalty Distribution**: Smart contracts can automatically execute royalty payments to authors whenever their NFTs are sold or accessed. This automation ensures timely and accurate payments, eliminating the need for intermediaries.
2. **Transparency and Accountability**: Blockchain technology provides a transparent and immutable record of all transactions. Authors can verify the sales and usage of their NFTs, ensuring they receive the correct royalties.
3. **Customizable Royalty Structures**: Authors can customize the terms of the smart contract to suit their specific royalty requirements. This includes setting different royalty rates for primary sales, secondary market resales, and other usage scenarios.

Best Practices for Royalty Tracking and Payments

1. **Understand Smart Contracts**: Authors should familiarize themselves with how smart contracts work and the benefits they offer. Online courses, tutorials, and articles can provide a solid foundation.
2. **Define Royalty Terms**: Authors should clearly define the royalty terms in the smart contract, including the percentage of royalties, the scenarios in which they apply, and any other relevant conditions.
3. **Consult with Experts**: Consulting with blockchain and smart contract experts can help authors create effective and legally sound royalty agreements. Experts can provide guidance on customizing smart contracts to meet specific needs.
4. **Monitor Transactions**: Authors should regularly monitor the transactions recorded on the blockchain to ensure they receive the correct royalties. This transparency allows authors to verify sales and usage and address any discrepancies.

Case Study: Automating Royalty Payments with Smart Contracts

An author publishes an electronic book as an NFT and uses a smart contract to automate royalty tracking and distribution. The smart contract specifies that the author will receive a 10% royalty on all primary sales and a 5% royalty on all secondary market resales.

Whenever the NFT is sold, the smart contract automatically executes the royalty payment, transferring the specified percentage to the author's wallet. The blockchain ledger provides a transparent record of all transactions, allowing the author to verify the sales and ensure they receive the correct royalties.

By leveraging smart contracts, the author ensures timely and accurate royalty payments, eliminates the need for intermediaries, and benefits from ongoing revenue opportunities in the secondary market.

Leveraging smart contracts for royalty tracking and payments offers authors a transparent and automated solution to ensure they receive fair compensation for their work. By understanding smart contracts, defining clear royalty terms, consulting with experts, and monitoring transactions, authors can maximize their earnings and maintain control over their digital assets. Embracing these best practices can help authors streamline royalty management and achieve financial success in the digital space.

27
Scalability and Transaction Costs

Authors should consider the scalability and transaction costs associated with blockchain networks. Depending on the chosen blockchain, there may be limitations on the number of transactions that can be processed efficiently. Authors should assess the scalability of the blockchain network to ensure it can handle the potential demand for their electronic books.

Understanding Scalability and Transaction Costs

1. **Scalability**: Scalability refers to the ability of a blockchain network to handle a large number of transactions efficiently. Authors should choose a blockchain network that can scale to meet the demand for their NFTs without compromising performance.
2. **Transaction Costs**: Transaction costs, also known as gas fees, are fees paid to process transactions on the blockchain. Authors should consider the transaction costs associated with minting, selling, and transferring NFTs, as high fees can impact profitability.

Best Practices for Managing Scalability and Transaction Costs

1. **Choose a Scalable Blockchain**: Authors should choose a blockchain network that offers high scalability and can handle a large volume of transactions efficiently. Researching and comparing different blockchain networks can help identify the best option.
2. **Monitor Network Congestion**: Network congestion can lead to increased transaction costs and delays. Authors

should monitor the blockchain network for congestion and choose times when the network is less busy to minimize costs.

3. **Optimize Smart Contracts**: Optimizing smart contracts can reduce transaction costs. Authors should work with blockchain experts to ensure their smart contracts are efficient and cost-effective.
4. **Consider Layer 2 Solutions**: Layer 2 solutions, such as sidechains and off-chain scaling techniques, can help reduce transaction costs and improve scalability. Authors should explore these solutions to enhance the performance of their NFTs.

Case Study: Managing Scalability and Transaction Costs for NFTs

An author decides to mint and sell their electronic book as an NFT. They research various blockchain networks and choose one known for its high scalability and low transaction costs.

To minimize transaction costs, the author monitors the network for congestion and chooses to mint and sell their NFTs during times of low activity. They also work with a blockchain expert to optimize their smart contracts, ensuring they are efficient and cost-effective.

Additionally, the author explores Layer 2 solutions to further reduce transaction costs and enhance scalability. By implementing these best practices, the author successfully manages scalability and transaction costs, maximizing profitability and ensuring a smooth user experience.

Managing scalability and transaction costs is crucial for the success of NFTs. By choosing a scalable blockchain, monitoring network congestion, optimizing smart contracts, and exploring Layer 2 solutions, authors can ensure efficient and cost-effective transactions. Embracing these best practices can help authors maximize profitability and maintain a positive user experience in the digital space.

28
Backup and Recovery

While blockchain technology provides resilience against data loss or tampering, authors should still have backup and recovery mechanisms in place. It's important to have redundant copies of their electronic books stored securely to mitigate the risk of losing access to their works due to unforeseen circumstances.

Ensuring Backup and Recovery for NFTs

1. **Redundant Copies**: Authors should maintain redundant copies of their electronic books and associated metadata. These copies should be stored securely in multiple locations to ensure data availability and protection against loss.
2. **Off-Chain Storage**: Off-chain storage solutions, such as decentralized storage networks and cloud services, can provide additional backup and recovery options. Authors should consider using these solutions to store redundant copies of their content.
3. **Regular Backups**: Regular backups are essential to ensure data integrity and availability. Authors should establish a routine backup schedule to create and store redundant copies of their electronic books and NFTs.

Best Practices for Backup and Recovery

1. **Use Multiple Storage Solutions**: Authors should use a combination of on-chain and off-chain storage solutions to create redundant copies of their electronic books and

NFTs. This approach ensures data availability and protection against loss.

2. **Implement Encryption**: Encrypting backup copies can enhance data security and protect against unauthorized access. Authors should consider using encryption techniques to safeguard their backups.
3. **Test Recovery Procedures**: Testing recovery procedures is crucial to ensure that backups can be restored successfully in the event of data loss. Authors should regularly test their recovery processes to verify data integrity and availability.
4. **Consult with Experts**: Consulting with data storage and recovery experts can provide valuable insights and guidance. Experts can help authors implement effective backup and recovery strategies to protect their content.

Case Study: Implementing Backup and Recovery for NFTs

An author decides to tokenize their electronic book as an NFT and implement backup and recovery mechanisms to protect their content. They create redundant copies of the electronic book and associated metadata, storing them securely in multiple locations.

The author uses a combination of on-chain and off-chain storage solutions, including decentralized storage networks and cloud services, to ensure data availability and protection against loss. They also implement encryption techniques to safeguard their backups.

To ensure data integrity, the author establishes a routine backup schedule and regularly tests their recovery procedures. By consulting with data storage and recovery experts, the author implements effective backup and recovery strategies, ensuring the protection and availability of their content.

NFT and Blockchain Essentials

Implementing backup and recovery mechanisms is essential for protecting electronic books and NFTs. By maintaining redundant copies, using multiple storage solutions, implementing encryption, testing recovery procedures, and consulting with experts, authors can ensure data availability and protection against loss. Embracing these best practices can help authors safeguard their content and maintain continuity in the digital space.

29
User Experience

Authors should prioritize the user experience when utilizing blockchain for their electronic books. It's essential to ensure that readers have a seamless and intuitive experience when accessing and reading the books on blockchain platforms. User feedback and continuous improvement efforts can help enhance the overall user experience.

Enhancing User Experience with Blockchain

1. **Seamless Access**: Authors should ensure that readers can easily access and purchase their electronic books on blockchain platforms. A user-friendly interface and clear instructions can enhance the purchasing experience.
2. **Intuitive Navigation**: Intuitive navigation is crucial for a positive user experience. Authors should choose platforms that offer clear and simple navigation, making it easy for readers to browse and access their electronic books.
3. **Responsive Design**: A responsive design ensures that the platform is accessible on various devices, including desktops, tablets, and smartphones. Authors should choose platforms that offer a responsive design to provide a consistent user experience across different devices.
4. **Customer Support**: Providing excellent customer support can enhance the user experience and address any issues or concerns. Authors should choose platforms that offer reliable customer support to assist readers with any questions or problems.

Best Practices for User Experience

1. **Optimize Platform Selection**: Choosing the right platform is crucial for ensuring a positive user experience. Authors should select platforms that offer seamless access, intuitive navigation, and responsive design.
2. **Gather User Feedback**: Gathering user feedback is essential for understanding the needs and preferences of readers. Authors should actively seek feedback and use it to make improvements to the user experience.
3. **Continuously Improve**: Continuous improvement efforts can help enhance the user experience over time. Authors should regularly review and update their content and platform settings to ensure a positive and engaging experience for readers.
4. **Engage with Readers**: Engaging with readers through the platform can provide valuable insights and build a sense of community. Authors should respond to questions, participate in discussions, and provide updates to keep readers informed and engaged.

Case Study: Enhancing User Experience for NFTs

An author decides to tokenize their electronic book as an NFT and prioritize the user experience. They choose a blockchain platform known for its user-friendly interface, intuitive navigation, and responsive design.

To optimize the user experience, the author gathers feedback from readers and uses it to make improvements. They implement clear instructions for purchasing and accessing the NFT, ensuring a seamless experience.

The author also engages with readers through the platform, responding to questions and providing updates. This approach enhances the user experience and builds a sense of community around the electronic book.

Prioritizing the user experience is crucial for the success of NFTs. By choosing the right platform, optimizing access and navigation, gathering user feedback, continuously improving, and engaging with readers, authors can ensure a positive and engaging experience for their audience. Embracing these best practices can help authors create a seamless and intuitive user experience in the digital space.

30
Legal and Regulatory Considerations

Authors should be aware of any legal and regulatory implications when using blockchain for their electronic books. Intellectual property rights, copyright laws, and data protection regulations may vary across jurisdictions. Seeking legal advice to ensure compliance with relevant laws and regulations is crucial.

Navigating Legal and Regulatory Considerations

1. **Intellectual Property Rights**: Authors must ensure they have the necessary rights to tokenize and sell their electronic books as NFTs. This includes verifying ownership, clearing any copyright or licensing issues, and understanding the legal implications of tokenizing intellectual property.
2. **Data Protection Regulations**: Data protection regulations, such as the General Data Protection Regulation (GDPR) in Europe, may impact the use of blockchain technology. Authors should understand the data protection requirements and ensure compliance with relevant regulations.
3. **Tax Implications**: Selling NFTs may have tax implications, including income tax, capital gains tax, and sales tax. Authors must understand their tax obligations and ensure proper reporting and payment of taxes related to NFT transactions.

Best Practices for Legal and Regulatory Compliance

1. **Seek Legal Advice**: Consulting with legal professionals who specialize in intellectual property and blockchain technology is crucial. Legal experts can provide guidance on copyright, licensing, data protection, and tax compliance.
2. **Understand Jurisdictional Differences**: Legal and regulatory requirements may vary across jurisdictions. Authors should understand the specific requirements in their country and any other jurisdictions where their NFTs may be sold.
3. **Create Clear Agreements**: Authors should create clear and detailed licensing agreements that outline the terms and conditions of the NFT sale. These agreements should specify the rights granted to the NFT holder, usage limitations, and any royalties or revenue-sharing arrangements.
4. **Maintain Accurate Records**: Keeping accurate records of NFT transactions is essential for legal and tax compliance. Authors should maintain detailed records of sales, income, expenses, and royalties to ensure proper reporting and compliance.

Case Study: Navigating Legal and Regulatory Considerations for NFTs

An author decides to tokenize their electronic book as an NFT and seeks legal advice to navigate the legal and regulatory implications. They consult with a legal professional who specializes in intellectual property and blockchain technology.

The legal professional helps the author verify ownership, clear any copyright issues, and create a detailed licensing agreement. The agreement outlines the terms and conditions of the NFT sale, including usage rights and royalties.

NFT and Blockchain Essentials

To ensure compliance with data protection regulations, the author understands the requirements of the GDPR and implements necessary measures to protect personal data. They also seek tax advice to understand their tax obligations and ensure proper reporting and payment of taxes related to NFT transactions.

By seeking legal and tax advice, understanding jurisdictional differences, creating clear agreements, and maintaining accurate records, the author ensures compliance with relevant laws and regulations. This approach helps the author navigate the legal and regulatory landscape and protect their rights.

Navigating legal and regulatory considerations is crucial for authors using blockchain technology. By seeking legal advice, understanding jurisdictional differences, creating clear agreements, and maintaining accurate records, authors can ensure compliance with relevant laws and regulations. Embracing these best practices can help authors protect their rights and achieve success in the digital space.

31
Continuous Learning and Adaptation

The NFT space is constantly evolving, with new trends, technologies, and market developments emerging regularly. For authors to stay competitive and seize new opportunities, continuous learning and adaptation are essential. This chapter explores best practices for staying informed and adapting to changes in the NFT space.

Embracing Continuous Learning

1. **Stay Informed**: Authors should stay informed about the latest trends, technologies, and market developments in the NFT space. Following industry news, reading articles, and participating in online forums can provide valuable insights.
2. **Attend Events and Webinars**: Attending industry events, conferences, and webinars can help authors learn from experts, network with peers, and stay up-to-date with the latest developments. These events provide opportunities for learning and growth.
3. **Engage with the Community**: Engaging with the NFT community can provide valuable insights and feedback. Authors should participate in discussions, ask questions, and learn from the experiences of others in the community.
4. **Experiment and Innovate**: Authors should be open to experimenting with new ideas and innovating in their approach to NFTs. Trying new strategies, exploring different revenue models, and adapting to changing market conditions can help authors stay competitive.

Best Practices for Continuous Learning and Adaptation

1. **Set Learning Goals**: Authors should set specific learning goals to stay focused and motivated. This can include learning about new technologies, understanding market trends, or improving skills related to NFTs and blockchain.
2. **Create a Learning Plan**: Developing a learning plan can help authors stay organized and track their progress. The plan should outline the resources, events, and activities that will help achieve their learning goals.
3. **Seek Mentorship and Guidance**: Finding mentors or seeking guidance from experienced individuals in the NFT space can provide valuable insights and support. Mentors can offer advice, share experiences, and help authors navigate challenges.
4. **Adapt to Changes**: Authors should be flexible and willing to adapt to changes in the NFT space. This includes staying open to new ideas, learning from failures, and continuously improving their approach.

Case Study: Embracing Continuous Learning and Adaptation

An author decides to embrace continuous learning and adaptation to stay competitive in the NFT space. They set specific learning goals, such as understanding new blockchain technologies and exploring innovative revenue models.

The author creates a learning plan that includes attending industry conferences, participating in webinars, and reading articles about the latest trends. They also engage with the NFT community, participating in online discussions and seeking feedback from peers.

To stay flexible and adapt to changes, the author experiments with different strategies and revenue models, learning from their successes and failures. They seek guidance from mentors who provide valuable insights and support.

By embracing continuous learning and adaptation, the author stays informed about the latest developments, improves their skills, and remains competitive in the NFT space. This approach helps them seize new opportunities and achieve long-term success.

Continuous learning and adaptation are essential for authors to stay competitive and seize new opportunities in the NFT space. By setting learning goals, creating a learning plan, seeking mentorship, and adapting to changes, authors can stay informed and continuously improve their approach. Embracing these best practices can help authors navigate the evolving NFT landscape and achieve success in the digital space.

32
Future Opportunities

The digital landscape is rapidly evolving, and emerging technologies like blockchain and NFTs are opening up new possibilities for authors. Embracing these technologies positions authors at the forefront of innovation, allowing them to explore novel revenue models and creative opportunities. This chapter explores the potential future opportunities for authors in the NFT and blockchain space.

Exploring Future Opportunities with NFTs and Blockchain

As blockchain technology and NFTs continue to develop, authors can experiment with new ways to monetize their work, engage with their audience, and enhance their creative output. Staying informed about emerging trends and technologies can help authors seize new opportunities and remain competitive in the digital publishing world.

Potential Future Opportunities for Authors

1. **Innovative Revenue Models**: Authors can explore new revenue models such as subscription-based access to exclusive content, tiered pricing for different levels of engagement, and dynamic pricing based on demand and scarcity.
2. **Collaborative Projects**: Blockchain technology enables collaborative projects where multiple authors, artists, and creators can work together to produce unique and innovative content. NFTs can represent shared ownership and revenue distribution among collaborators.

3. **Interactive Storytelling**: The integration of interactive and multimedia elements within electronic books can create immersive storytelling experiences. Authors can experiment with augmented reality (AR), virtual reality (VR), and gamification to engage readers in new and exciting ways.
4. **Tokenized Communities**: Authors can create tokenized communities where fans and readers can participate in the creation and promotion of new works. Token holders can have voting rights, access to exclusive content, and opportunities to collaborate with the author.
5. **Decentralized Publishing Platforms**: Emerging decentralized publishing platforms leverage blockchain technology to provide authors with more control over their work and revenue. These platforms eliminate traditional gatekeepers, allowing authors to publish and distribute their work directly to readers.

Case Study: Experimenting with Innovative Revenue Models

An author decides to experiment with a subscription-based revenue model using NFTs. They create a series of NFTs that grant subscribers access to exclusive monthly content, including new chapters, behind-the-scenes insights, and interactive events.

Subscribers purchase the NFTs, which automatically renew each month through a smart contract. The author benefits from a steady stream of revenue and a dedicated subscriber base. The subscription model allows the author to engage with their readers on an ongoing basis, providing fresh and exclusive content that keeps subscribers excited and invested.

The future opportunities for authors in the NFT and blockchain space are vast and varied. By staying informed about emerging trends and technologies, authors can experiment with innovative revenue models, collaborative projects, interactive storytelling, and tokenized communities. Embracing these opportunities can help authors remain competitive, engage with their audience in new ways, and maximize the potential of their creative works. As the digital landscape continues to evolve, authors who leverage NFTs and blockchain technology will be well-positioned to thrive in the future of digital publishing.

About the Author

B Alan Bourgeois began his writing journey at age 12, crafting screenplays for *Adam-12* as an outlet to develop his style. While he never submitted these works, the experience fueled his passion for storytelling. After following the conventional advice of pursuing a stable career, Bourgeois rediscovered his love for writing in 1989 through a community college class, leading to his first published short story. Since then, he has written over 48 short stories, published more than 10 books, including the award-winning *Extinguishing the Light*, and made his mark in the publishing world.

Recognizing the challenges authors face, Bourgeois founded Creative House Press in the early 2000s, publishing 60 books by other authors in five years and gaining insights into the industry's marketing needs. In 2011, he launched the Texas Authors Association, which grew to include two nonprofits promoting Texas writers and literacy. He also created innovative programs like the Lone Star Festival and short story contests for students, and in 2016, the Authors Marketing Event, offering a groundbreaking Certification program for book marketing expertise.

Despite setbacks during the COVID-19 pandemic, Bourgeois adapted by launching the Authors School of Business, providing essential tools for authors to succeed as "Authorpreneurs." As publishing evolves, he has explored NFTs as a potential revenue stream for writers. With decades of experience, Bourgeois remains a driving force in the literary community, committed to helping authors thrive in a changing industry.

Bourgeois is currently the director of the Texas Authors Museum & Institute of History, based in Austin, Texas

Other Books by the Author in this Series

Y'all Write: A Month-Long Guide to Achieving Your Writing Goals

Unlock your creative potential with *Y'all Write: A Month of Writing Celebration and Growth*! This guide offers tips, motivation, and tools to help writers of all levels set goals, build momentum, and embrace the joy of storytelling.

Author's Roadmap to Success: Proven Strategies for Thriving in Publishing

Unlock the secrets to literary success with *Author's Roadmap to Success: Proven Strategies for Thriving in Publishing*. This essential guide provides actionable strategies to help writers build strong habits, master self-publishing, and thrive in their writing careers.

The Writer's Self-Care Guide: Top Ten Steps to Balance and Thrive

Transform your writing journey with *The Writer's Self-Care Guide: Top Ten Steps to Balance and Thrive*. This practical guide offers actionable steps to nurture your creativity, set boundaries, and achieve a balanced, fulfilling writing life.

Top Ten Keys for Successful Writing and Productivity

Unlock your writing potential with *Top Ten Keys for Successful Writing and Productivity*. This guide offers actionable strategies to build consistent habits, manage time effectively, and produce high-quality work to elevate your writing

Mastering Research: Top Ten Steps to Research Like a Pro

Elevate your writing with *Mastering Research: Top Ten Steps to Research Like a Pro*. This essential guide provides practical tools and techniques to conduct thorough, credible research and seamlessly integrate it into your work.

Character Chronicles: Crafting Depth and Consistency in Creative Projects

Bring your characters to life with *Character Chronicles: Crafting Depth and Consistency in Creative Projects*. This essential guide reveals professional techniques to develop authentic, complex characters that resonate across any creative medium.

Editing Essentials: Your Guide to Finding the Perfect Editor

Transform your manuscript with *Editing Essentials: Your Guide to Finding the Perfect Editor*. This guide provides practical steps to identify, evaluate, and collaborate with the ideal editor to elevate your writing.

NFT and Blockchain Essentials

AI Programs Apps Authors Should Use

Revolutionize your writing with *Top Ten AI Programs Authors Should Use*. This guide explores powerful AI tools like Grammarly and Scrivener, offering practical tips to enhance creativity, productivity, and efficiency.

The Business of Writing

Master the publishing world with *Unlocking the Business of Writing*. This essential guide provides expert advice and practical tips to build your author platform, maximize royalties, and turn your passion into a thriving career.

Creating an Effective Book Cover

Create a book cover that captivates readers with *Top Ten Keys to Creating an Effective Book Cover*. This guide offers expert tips and practical advice on design, branding, and marketing to make your book stand out.

Mastering the Art of the Sales Pitch

Master the art of the sales pitch with *Mastering the Art of the Sales Pitch*. This guide provides essential strategies to captivate your audience, highlight your book's value, and drive its success.

Publishing Issues Authors Deal With

Overcome publishing challenges with *Publishing Issues Authors Deal With*. This guide offers practical strategies and expert insights to help you navigate rejection, editing, marketing, and more to achieve your publishing dreams.

The Indie Author Advantage: Mastering Control, Royalties, and Reach for Self-Publishing Success

Thrive as an indie author with *The Indie Author Advantage: Mastering Control, Royalties, and Reach for Self-Publishing Success*. This guide offers actionable strategies to retain creative control, maximize royalties, and reach a global audience.

Mastering Amazon Publishing: A Comprehensive Guide to Success for Indie Authors

Achieve self-publishing success with *Mastering Amazon Publishing: A Comprehensive Guide to Success for Indie Authors*. This guide provides proven strategies to navigate KDP, boost visibility, and maximize earnings for your books.

Marketing Essentials for Authors: Proven Strategies to Boost Book Sales

Boost your book sales with *Top Ten Marketing Essentials for Authors: Proven Strategies to Promote Your Book*. This guide combines traditional and digital marketing tactics to help authors effectively connect with readers and turn their books into bestsellers.

Marketing Mastery: Avoiding Common Mistakes for Authors

Master book marketing with *Marketing Mastery: Avoiding Common Mistakes for Authors*. This guide offers actionable advice to help authors connect with readers, build a strong online presence, and achieve their publishing goals.

The Author Branding Blueprint

Elevate your writing career with *Author Brand Mastery: A Comprehensive Guide to Building and Sustaining Your Unique Identity*. This guide provides practical steps to define your brand, build a professional presence, and connect meaningfully with your audience.

Reader Magnet: Top Strategies for Building an Engaged Reader Community

Build a loyal reader community with *Reader Magnet: Top Strategies for Building an Engaged Reader Community*. This guide offers actionable strategies to connect with readers, create exclusive content, and turn your audience into passionate advocates.

Author Platform Mastery: A Comprehensive Guide to Building, Monetizing, and Growing Your Audience

Build your literary empire with *Author Platform Mastery: A Comprehensive Guide to Building, Monetizing, and Growing Your Audience*. This essential guide offers practical strategies to define your brand, engage readers, and expand your reach.

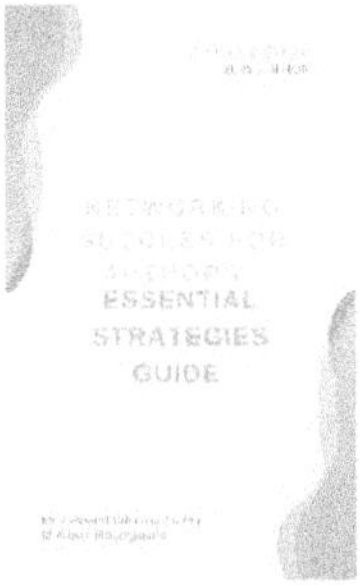

Networking Success for Authors: Essential Strategies Guide

Achieve your literary goals with *Networking Success for Authors: Essential Strategies Guide*. This practical roadmap offers strategies to build meaningful connections, promote your work, and create a supportive community for lasting success.

Write, Publish, Market: The Ultimate Handbook for Author Success

ISBN:

Master the modern publishing landscape with *Write, Publish, Market: The Ultimate Handbook for Author Success*. This guide provides actionable strategies to build your author brand, attract readers, and achieve long-term success in your writing career.

NFT and Blockchain Essentials

Mastering Interviews: Essential Tips for Authors' Success

Excel in interviews with *Mastering Interviews: Essential Tips for Authors' Success*. This guide offers practical advice to confidently promote your work, connect with audiences, and turn every interview into a memorable success.

Mastering Event Presentations: Avoiding Common Author Mistakes

Captivate your audience with *Mastering Event Presentations: Avoiding Common Author Mistakes*. This guide offers practical strategies to avoid pitfalls, engage your audience, and deliver impactful presentations that boost your confidence and connect with readers.

Survival Strategies for Indie Authors: Overcoming Challenges and Achieving Success

Thrive as an indie author with *Survival Strategies for Indie Authors: Overcoming Challenges and Achieving Success*. This guide provides practical advice and actionable tips to overcome obstacles, enhance your skills, and achieve your publishing goals.

Empowering Authors: Top Ten Strategies for Writing Success and Career Growth

Achieve your writing dreams with *Empowering Authors: Top Ten Strategies for Writing Success and Career Growth*. This guide offers practical advice and proven strategies to build habits, refine your craft, and grow your author career with confidence.

The Sacred Connection

Infuse your writing with mindfulness and purpose through *Creating with Spirit: The Sacred Art of Writing and Publishing*. This guide transforms your creative journey into a spiritual practice, empowering you to inspire readers and overcome challenges with authenticity and intention.

Beyond the Basics: Advanced Strategies for Indie Author Success

ISBN:

Elevate your indie publishing career with *Beyond the Basics: Advanced Strategies for Indie Author Success*. This guide offers actionable tips and strategies to diversify income, engage readers, and build a sustainable, thriving career.

NFT and Blockchain Essentials

The AI Author: Embracing the Future of Fiction

Embrace the future of storytelling with *The AI Author: Balancing Efficiency and Creativity in Fiction Writing*. This guide helps authors harness AI to boost productivity and creativity while preserving the emotional depth and artistry of creating.

The Non-Fiction Nexus: Balancing AI and Human Insight in the Future of Writing

Elevate your non-fiction writing with *The Non-Fiction Nexus: Balancing AI and Human Insight in the Future of Writing*. This guide shows how to harness AI's efficiency while preserving the creativity and ethical judgment that make your work truly impactful.

Authorship Reimagined: NFTs and Blockchain Essentials

ISBN:

Embrace the future of publishing with *NFT and Blockchain Essentials for Authors' Success*. This guide explains how blockchain and NFTs can protect your work, automate royalties, and expand your audience while maximizing revenue.

Adapting Success: Your Book's Journey to Film

Turn your book into a cinematic sensation with *From Page to Screen: A Step-by-Step Guide to Adapting Your Book into a Blockbuster Film.* This guide provides practical advice and industry insights to help you navigate the adaptation process and bring your story to life on the big screen.

Beyond the Basics: Advanced Strategies for Indie Author Success

Elevate your indie publishing career with this ultimate guide to mastering advanced strategies in writing, marketing, and global distribution. Packed with actionable tips and real-world examples, it empowers authors to balance creativity with entrepreneurship and build sustainable, thriving careers.

2026: The Ultimate Year for Indie Authors

Make 2026 your breakthrough year with *The Ultimate Year for Indie Authors*. This guide offers practical strategies to optimize publishing, leverage social media, and achieve unparalleled success in your indie author journey.

www.ingramcontent.com/pod-product-compliance
Lightning Source LLC
LaVergne TN
LVHW010806110225
803462LV00001B/187